A REPORT FROM THE FRONT LINES

A REPORT FROM THE FRONT LINES

Conversations on Public Theology

∽

A Festschrift in Honor of
Robert Benne

Edited by

Michael Shahan

William B. Eerdmans Publishing Company
Grand Rapids, Michigan / Cambridge, U.K.

Published 2009 by
Wm. B. Eerdmans Publishing Co.
2140 Oak Industrial Drive N.E., Grand Rapids, Michigan 49505 /
P.O. Box 163, Cambridge CB3 9PU U.K.

Printed in the United States of America

15 14 13 12 11 10 09   7 6 5 4 3 2 1

Library of Congress Cataloging-in-Publication Data

A report from the front lines: conversations on public theology:
a festschrift in honor of Robert Benne / edited by Michael Shahan.
p.   cm.
Includes bibliographical references.
ISBN 978-0-8028-4863-5 (pbk.: alk. paper)
1. Christian sociology — Lutheran Church.
2. Christian ethics — Lutheran authors.
3. Two kingdoms (Lutheran theology)
4. Church and state — Lutheran Church.
5. Christianity and politics — Lutheran Church.
I. Shahan, Michael.   II. Benne, Robert.

BT738.R455   2009
261 — dc22

2008037329

www.eerdmans.com

Contents

CONTRIBUTORS   vii

Introduction   xi
John R. Stumme

THE IMPERATIVE OF A PUBLIC THEOLOGY

The Attack on Transcendence and the Response of Robert Benne   3
Michael Shahan

The Crux of Christianity's Case: The Resurrection of Jesus   23
Carl E. Braaten

A Cultural Disorder: C. S. Lewis and the Abolition of Man   35
Jean Bethke Elshtain

Attending to the Business That Is Ours   47
Richard John Neuhaus

THE LUTHERAN NECESSITY IN PUBLIC THEOLOGY

The Lutheran Difference   55
James Nuechterlein

The Lutheran Corrective 66
  Gilbert Meilaender

What Lutherans Have to Offer 76
  Mark A. Noll

CONTESTED ISSUES IN PUBLIC THEOLOGY

Luther and Liberalism 89
  Paul R. Hinlicky

The Public Theologian as Connected Critic: The Case of Central
European Churches 105
  Ronald F. Thiemann

Persuasion and Indoctrination in Lutheran Colleges 120
  Gerald R. McDermott

The Recovery of Moral and Religious Truth in the University 141
  Donald D. Schmeltekopf and Michael D. Beaty

Religious Perspectives on Democratic Capitalism 160
  Joseph A. Swanson

Contributors

MICHAEL D. BEATY is Professor of Philosophy and chair of the Department of Philosophy, Baylor University. His published works include *Christian Theism and Moral Philosophy* (ed.); *Christian Theism and the Problems of Philosophy* (ed.); and others on secularization and American universities. He has directed the Institute for Faith and Learning at Baylor University.

CARL E. BRAATEN is Professor of Systematic Theology Emeritus, Lutheran School of Theology at Chicago. With Robert Jenson, he co-founded the Center for Catholic and Evangelical Theology. His books include *Principles of Lutheran Theology; The Future of God;* the two-volume *Christian Dogmatics* (with Robert Jenson); *No Other Gospel;* and many others.

JEAN BETHKE ELSHTAIN is Laura Spelman Rockefeller Professor of Social and Political Ethics in the Chicago Divinity School; she also serves in the Department of Political Science and the Committee on International Relations at the University of Chicago. Her recent books include *Just War against Terror* (2003) and *Jane Addams and the Dream of American Democracy* (2002).

PAUL R. HINLICKY is Tise Professor of Lutheran Studies at Roanoke College. He is an internationally known theologian who has published numerous articles and is editor and author (with Dennis Bielfeldt and Mickey Mattox) of *The Substance of the Faith: Luther on Doctrinal Theology* (Fortress, 2008) and author of *Paths Not Taken: Fates of Theology from Luther through Leibniz* (Eerdmans, forthcoming). An ordained minister of the Evangelical Lutheran Church in America, he is also the former editor of the *Lutheran Forum* and associate editor of *Pro Ecclesia*. He came to Roanoke College after teaching theology for six years at Jan Comenius University in Bratislava, Slovakia.

GERALD R. MCDERMOTT is Professor of Religion at Roanoke College. He is the author of many books, including *One Holy and Happy Society: The Public Theology of Jonathan Edwards* (Penn State Press); *Jonathan Edwards Confronts the Gods* (Oxford University Press); *God's Rivals: Why Has God Allowed Different Religions?* (InterVarsity Press); and, with Robert Millett, *Claiming Christ: A Mormon-Evangelical Debate* (Brazos Press). He is now editing *Understanding Jonathan Edwards* (Oxford University Press) and the *Oxford Handbook of Evangelical Theology* (Oxford University Press).

GILBERT MEILAENDER is Phyllis and Richard Duesenberg Professor of Christian Ethics, Valparaiso University and Fellow of the Hastings Center. Since its inception in 2002 he has been a member of the President's Council on Bioethics. His books include *The Way That Leads There: Augustinian Reflections on the Christian Life* (Eerdmans, 2006) and *The Oxford Handbook of Theological Ethics* (2005) (co-editor).

RICHARD JOHN NEUHAUS, a prominent Catholic priest and public theologian, is Editor in Chief of *First Things* and the founder of Religion and Public Life, an inter-religious research and education center. Among his books are *The Naked Public Square* (1984), *The Catholic Moment* (1987), and *Catholic Matters* (2006).

MARK NOLL is Francis A. McAnaney Professor of History, University of Notre Dame, and a major interpreter of evangelicalism. His recent publications include *The Civil War as a Theological Crisis* (2006); *The Rise of Evangelicalism: The Age of Edwards, Whitefield and the Wesleys* (2004); and *America's God, from Jonathan Edwards to Abraham Lincoln* (2002).

JAMES NUECHTERLEIN is Senior Fellow of the Institute on Religion and Public Life. He was formerly Editor of *First Things* and *The Cresset;* and he was also formerly Professor of American Studies and Political Thought at Valparaiso University.

Donald D. Schmeltekopf is Provost Emeritus of Baylor University and Professor and Director of the Center for Ministry Effectiveness and Educational Leadership, Baylor. He is the editor of four books on the subject of Christianity and higher education.

Michael Shahan, an ordained pastor of the Evangelical Lutheran Church in America, is Book Review Editor, *Journal of Lutheran Ethics* and a freelance writer in Nashville, Tennessee.

John R. Stumme is former Director of Studies for the Church in Society, Evangelical Lutheran Church in America. He is co-editor with Robert W. Tuttle of *Church and State: Lutheran Perspectives* and co-editor with Karen Bloomquist of *The Promise of Lutheran Ethics*. His articles include "Pursuing Peace without Illusions," in *WORD & WORLD*.

Joseph A. Swanson is Clinical Professor of Finance, Kellogg School of Management, Northwestern University. He is also the owner and president of Joseph A. Swanson and Co. of Milwaukee, Wisconsin.

Ronald F. Thiemann is Bussey Professor of Theology at Harvard Divinity School, Faculty Associate of the Weatherhead Center for International Affairs, and Faculty Fellow at the J.F.K. School's Hauser Center for Nonprofit Organizations. An ordained Lutheran pastor, he has authored *Revelation and Theology: The Gospel as Narrated Promise; Constructing a Public Theology: The Church in a Pluralistic Culture;* and *Religion in Public Life: A Dilemma for Democracy.*

Introduction

JOHN R. STUMME

"Public theology, I think, refers to the *engagement* of a living religious tradition with its public environment — the economic, political, and cultural
spheres of our common life."[1] So writes Robert Benne in *The Paradoxical
Vision*, one of the most significant proposals for Christian public theology
in recent decades. Benne's understanding of public theology captures well
the intent and content of the dozen essays in this book dedicated to honor-
ing him on his seventieth birthday. Here prominent thinkers demonstrate
the liveliness of the Christian tradition as they engage public life in themes
that Benne has addressed in his vocation as a public theologian.

The term "public theology" may trace the origin of its current usage to
the last decades of the twentieth century, where it countered the notion that
Christian faith was a private matter without public significance. Yet according to Benne's broad understanding of the term, the reality of Christian public theology has been around since New Testament times. Christians learned
from the faith of Israel that God is sovereign over all of life, and therefore
they were called to engage the public world. Through the centuries this engagement has been driven by different theological perspectives and themes
and has taken many different — even opposing — forms and shapes, from
categorical rejection of the world to easy accommodation to it. This book
belongs to this ongoing conversation, and its essays contribute to the debate
over the theology and shape of this engagement in today's public world.

1. Robert Benne, *The Paradoxical Vision: A Public Theology for the Twenty-first Century*
(Minneapolis: Fortress Press, 1995), p. 4.

The authors in this book know well both the history of Christian public engagement and the challenges of our common life in the twenty-first century. They care both for the truth and vitality of the Christian witness as well as for the common good of society in its various spheres. They neither reject all contemporary culture nor accommodate to it but exhibit and call for a critical attitude that discerns when to say "no" and when to say "yes." Where our culture seeks to marginalize, dismiss, or domesticate religion, the authors place Christian faith in the public square. This presence serves culture by defending and extending human dignity, opposing notions that limit the idea of who belongs to the human family.

Like Benne himself, these authors are troubled by how Christian churches in our culture often are unable to nurture and transmit a living tradition that deeply shapes the life of their members and institutions. For these authors (as has been the case with Benne), this concern leads them to attend to core elements of Christian faith and morality and to seek the Church's renewal from the resources of the Great Tradition of catholic Christianity. They know that the intellectual component of public theology is crucial for the Church's faithful renewal.

The book's first section provides context and content for public theology today. Michael Shahan points to powerful currents in our culture that deny, indeed, attack transcendence and strive for a culture without God. "The real nub of today's culture wars," he writes, "is a contest between those who value the vertical dimension in religious commitment and those who substitute the horizontal in its place." Shahan places Benne in the forefront of those addressing this crisis in church and culture. He then introduces us to Benne's life and thought and shows how Benne has moved between the two poles of faithfulness to the Christian tradition and practical engagement with his cultural context.

In order to be Christian, public theology depends on the resurrection of Jesus. So argues Carl E. Braaten: "Without faith in the resurrection — let there be no mistake about it — Christianity will have morphed into a different religion." In the pluralistic public square, the resurrection identifies God as the one who raised Jesus from the dead. "The resurrection tells us who God is and which God is the true God among the gods and idols in the universe of religions." In making the case for the centrality of the resurrection for Christian faith and drawing out its implications for Christian life, Braaten highlights Benne's concern for the core of the Christian vision.

Benne has written that the most important religiously grounded principle for the political order is the sanctity of the person. Jean Bethke Elshtain supports this claim. She uses C. S. Lewis's *The Abolition of Man* to defend human dignity against attempts to narrow the definition of humanity "in the name of expanding choice and eliminating 'suffering.'" She finds that what Lewis had detected as a threat to humanity in his age's embrace of subjectivism is very much alive today and "undermining the ontological claims of human dignity that ground human rights." Her stunning illustrations strengthen her argument. Elshtain agrees with Lewis that there are certain objective, trans-cultural, universal ethical norms.

Richard John Neuhaus sees Benne's and his work as both aiming at "a renewal of Christian confidence in providing a morally informed philosophy for a more just and virtuous society in the tradition of liberal democracy." Neuhaus reflects on his important book *The Naked Public Square* now more than two decades after its 1984 publication. While then the phrase "religion and public life" was controversial, now it is widely accepted "that we cannot understand any society without engaging its cultural and religious dynamics." Neuhaus proposes both that our "constitutional order is not sustainable apart from the cultural, moral, and religious expression of the self-evident truths on which it is founded" and that political questions ought to be resolvable by moral reason that is accessible to all.

The second section of the book deals explicitly with Benne's own Lutheran tradition. Benne's writings are clearly marked by Lutheran themes and concern for Lutheran churches in the United States. He seeks to give a Lutheran "nudge" to political theology largely shaped by the Reformed tradition. It is fitting, therefore, that three authors focus on Lutheranism.

James Nuechterlein explores his own experiences "living and worshipping as a Lutheran" in a way that illumines both for Lutherans and non-Lutherans what it has meant for many to be a Lutheran in our time. According to Nuechterlein what is "distinctively Lutheran" is not the doctrine of justification but "the setting of that doctrine in a dialectical theological framework." The Lutheran dialectic, similar to Benne's "paradox," takes many forms that "fit the rough contrariness of our experience; they are at once contradictory and true." Nuechterlein's observations about Lutheran church bodies in the United States coincide with criticisms Benne has made of them in his books and in many occasional pieces.

Gilbert Meilaender takes a different approach and as a Lutheran argues for the limits of Lutheranism. Building on Søren Kierkegaard's contention that Lutheranism is "'a corrective made into the norm, the whole,'" Meilaender asserts that "we have too often sought to construct an entire theology on the basis of some supposed distinctively Lutheran insight — most generally, some version of the distinction between law and gospel, sin and grace." As a result Lutherans have not had much to say about the distinctive shape and form of the Christian life; instead of finding direction for the Christian life in the will of God, they have taken their behavioral cues from the world around them. Meilaender illustrates the importance of setting Lutheranism within the context of the larger catholic tradition with reference to abortion where the almost universal witness of the early church was "that the child in the womb is one of us from the time of conception," a witness affirmed by the Reformers.

Historian Mark A. Noll observes that "political activity by American Christian believers, especially evangelicals, has often been lacking exactly in those areas where Lutheran theology is strong." Noll, a Reformed theologian who has high praise for Benne's *The Paradoxical Vision*, outlines what Lutheran theology seems to offer in terms of motives, priorities, attitudes, and goals; yet, he writes, Lutheran practice has not fulfilled this promise. Noll offers various possible explanations on why Lutherans have exerted such scant positive effect on the course of political life.

Through his books and articles Benne has addressed many issues in "the economic, political, and cultural spheres of our common life." The essays in the third section of this book take up some of these issues. Paul R. Hinlicky, noting that Benne is both a classical liberal and a Lutheran, explores the meaning of freedom in these two traditions and their relationship. For Luther freedom is a gift from God, an event that comes from outside us. "What has this exclusively theological event to do with the struggle today for human freedom in the world? . . . I want to sort our way through some of these disputes." Hinlicky critiques modernized views of Luther and interprets liberalism to mean that "*liberty is secured as the minimum basis* for civilized life and the prospect of progress on the other values of equality and fraternity." Hinlicky draws again from Luther to propose that the church not the state is where fraternity is to be found.

Ronald F. Thiemann provides a model for the public theologian as "connected critic." His essay learns from and addresses central European churches in their struggles to create more responsible forms of citizenship. "Connected criticism of the public theologian oscillates between the poles of critique and connection, solitude and solidarity, alienation and authority. . . . This dialectic between commitment and critique is the identifying feature."

In distinction from other essays in this book, Joseph A. Swanson focuses directly on Benne's life and work, in particular on *The Ethic of Democratic Capitalism*. Swanson gives a vivid description of the context in which Benne wrote his ground-breaking book and outlines its contributions. "Benne got the economic system bet right, the first time in a long time that a theologian had done so in this field." Swanson points to the importance of cultural factors in economic growth and proposes that culture is the arena for the engagement of theology and economics in the twenty-first century.

Following in the path of Benne's *Quality with Soul,* the last two essays attend to religion in higher education. Gerald McDermott proposes "a new model for pedagogy in the Lutheran college classroom, one that can speak of faith without indoctrination." He criticizes the Lutheran academy for adopting uncritically narrow views of reason and knowledge from certain Enlightenment traditions, and he challenges the Enlightenment presumptions about fact and opinion, neutrality, and intellectual autonomy. He contends Western thinkers confused persuasion with indoctrination and lost the oratorical ideal, which stressed the need to pass traditions on to the uninitiated. McDermott calls for a balance between teaching a tradition and criticism of the tradition. Donald D. Schmeltekopf and Michael D. Beaty point to signs of the recovery of moral and religious truth in the university and then argue for this recovery. They "give support to a larger and, in fact, more traditional notion of the university, one that takes into account the full range of human experience, including in particular the moral and religious domains."

Readers of these essays will gain a new appreciation of how thinking rooted in the great Christian tradition engages its public environment vigorously and faithfully. They will find in them quality with soul. Readers will also gain a new appreciation of Robert Benne, an ordinary saint who in his vocation as a public theologian witnesses with courage and wisdom to the Gospel of Jesus Christ for the glory of God, Father, Son, and Holy Spirit.

The Imperative of a Public Theology

The Attack on Transcendence and the Response of Robert Benne

MICHAEL SHAHAN

The last king should be strangled with the entrails of the last priest.

There was a time when this bit of Enlightenment wisdom from the pen of Denis Diderot (1713-1784) would have brought a wry smile from the lips of a sophisticated believer. In the 1950s Christian belief occupied a secure enough position in American culture and social life that a typical mainstream Protestant pastor would have enjoyed the presumed joke behind this edgy and outrageous adage. Not anymore. Or, at least that shouldn't be the case.

Unlike the days of *Leave It to Beaver,* the intellectual furniture of the typical American's mind today does not automatically include an altar. Indeed, the notion that Christian faith should be forced to wear a warning label, and even to have some sort of sanction legislated against it, is becoming increasingly fashionable. While the anti-Christian animus of our time may not be expressed in such openly bloodthirsty terms as in the late eighteenth century, everyone is familiar with the anti-clerical, anti-Christian footprints of present-day American society. In the mainstream media, in the centers of higher learning, or in the courts, Christianity is taking a bit of a beating. Regardless of the well-documented sympathy toward Christianity by the American citizenry as a whole, within elite circles of opinion biblical religion has, to say the least, fallen on hard times. And, judged by the behavior of Church leaders, Christians are, by and large, taking it lying down.

Public theology seeks to address this rather grim state of affairs by uttering its voice on the public stage. A theology is public to the degree that it speaks a language common to the wider audience of society at large, about issues affecting that forum, yet does so in fidelity to its faith commitments. For Christians, a public theology assumes that the insights of the faith can be relevant for all, believer and unbeliever alike. Whether the subject is just war, genetic engineering, abortion, or the way we order our common life politically, a public theology will try to address common concerns out of a discrete system of belief.

This essay looks at one peculiar challenge to the faith arising from a culture that is increasingly hostile to Christianity. And it finds in the work of Robert Benne an exemplary model of authentic Christian public philosophy.

A Materialist Heart

It is more than coincidence that the anti-Christian Diderot foreshadowed Darwin's evolutionary theories as well as much contemporary speculation about natural selection. Both of these ideologies bring with them a materialist evaluation of human life. Further, this "humanist" thinker focused an inordinate amount of energy and bile on skewering conventional morality and the "superstitions" of the masses. If all this sounds strangely familiar, you need to understand that to look at Diderot is to see one side of ourselves.

Richard Dawkins, controversial scientist and unrelenting evolutionist (known as "Darwin's Rottweiler"), calls religion a "virus" and proclaims the teaching of faith to children a form of "child abuse." (The reader will note that very few voices of protest are heard in the mainstream media or in the commanding heights of our culture.) Indeed, Dawkins is in the vanguard of a sizeable movement in Western society dedicated to discrediting Christianity by pitting revelation against reason, and arguing the psychologically damaging effect of religion upon society. We would do well to recognize that this is not your granddad's version of "Christianity against culture": rather, it is a full-blown cult of godlessness disguised as "neutral" secularism, and pitted first against Christianity but finally against all religion. It is the logical outcome of having a "materialist heart."

While contemporary anti-religious zealotry cannot be laid directly at the doorstep of our eighteenth-century Jesuit-trained empiricist, Diderot, it is a fact that there are toxic ideas which have dogged Christianity over the centuries, and which refuse to die no matter how many times defeated on the battlefield of ideas. The perennial error of Gnosticism, a heresy which denigrates the flesh and offers release from the reality of this world, is a case in point. Its genetic footprint seems to miraculously appear wherever revisionists are trying to substitute an ersatz religion in place of Christianity or a "better" morality for the conventional one. Another is the ageless heresy of Arianism with its subordination of the second Person of the Godhead and its reduction of Jesus to the size of his admirers. Both of these ancient heresies have left their paw prints all over today's radical secularist crusade. And like them, neither will it go away easily.

Take the case of Diderot's crude materialist viewpoint, with its "oh, so sophisticated" skepticism about religion. No matter how many times it is slain in the arena of debate and logic, this heresy, too, will not cry "uncle." A materialist philosophy gives priority to the earthly over the spiritual, to the paramount influence of the economic and the social over the immaterial, to the natural over the transcendent. Whether explaining how the world is structured or how historians and social scientists should read the human drama, it agrees with Thomas Hobbes (1588-1679) that the sum and substance of reality is matter. To the determined materialist, man is exclusively and radically a material entity. There is no "soul," no heavenly realm, no God. This is a distinctly horizontal view of reality, and it precludes any intrusion by the vertical and transcendent dimension. Diderot is a faithful combatant of this school.

Religion as Contamination

The "permanent wear" quality of a materialist worldview is on display for the modern reader in the thought of the late Richard Rorty. Considered by many to be America's most important political theorist of the last generation, he was a self-confessed atheist who had little respect for religion as a source of real truth or commonly accepted values. A central theme of his thought is that the public arena — where citizens meet to do their collaborating and compromising, in short where the public business gets done — must be sterilized of the contamination of religion. His rationale: religion is a matter of the heart, not of the head. It arouses deep passions within the human breast, often leading to dissension if not war, and does not contribute constructively to intelligible discussion of matters pertaining to the commonweal. Therefore, religion must be kept at the margins of society, where it can provide whatever solace to individuals it has to offer, but where it is safely quarantined from infecting the public discussion of society's goals. According to this skeptical sage, such marginalization of religion would give America a better chance at achieving a fairer, more just society.

Rorty's estimate of religion's value has everything to do with his extreme proposal for saving the political realm. As he once phrased it: the Enlightenment "was right to suggest that religion is something that the human species would be better if it could outgrow."[1] While not publicly endorsing Diderot's drastic prescription for extirpating society of the Christian disease, he understands the frustrations behind the intolerant bias against religion. Essentially, his opinion — and that of many secularists today — is contained in the notion that humans would be better off worrying about the earthly well-being of their fellows than about some amorphous, ethereal relationship with a God who allegedly dwells in another realm. Before dismissing this as the odd ruminations of an obscure ivory tower academician, understand that this is the real agenda of many social activists today.

In a brief essay on atheists and citizenship, Richard John Neuhaus, in a book he co-edited[2] with George Weigel, identifies the intellectual beginnings of this antipathy toward religion with the inventor of analytic geometry, René Descartes (1596-1650). In the attempt to reach metaphysical conclusions possessing a mathematical kind of certainty, this "father of modern philosophy" employed a "procedural atheism" that accepted as true only that which could not reasonably be doubted. He thereby arrived at his well-known construction: "But as I was then minded to give myself entirely to the search for truth, I thought that what was required of me was . . . that I ought to reject as downright false all opinions which I could imagine to be in the least degree open to doubt . . . and noting that this

---

1. Jason Bofetti, "How Richard Rorty Found Religion," *First Things* 143 (May 2004): 24-30.

2. Richard John Neuhaus and George Weigel, *Being Christian Today: An American Conversation* (Washington, D.C.: Ethics and Public Policy Center, 1992). This is a remarkable compendium of essays marking the centenary of *Rerum Novarum*, the 1891 encyclical of Pope Leo XIII. Of incalculable influence on my argument in this chapter have been two essays in this volume: Max Stackhouse, "Liberalism Revisited: From Social Gospel to Public Theology," pp. 33-53; and Richard Neuhaus, "Can Atheists Be Good Citizens?" pp. 295-308.

truth *I think, therefore I am,* was so steadfast and so assured . . . I concluded that I might without scruple accept it as being the first principle."[3]

Neuhaus wonders what happened to this great philosopher of the "Cogito" that he forgot the crucial importance of doubt as a component of faith. By importing into our talk about God the notion that certainty must be restricted to what the human intellect can certify as sure, Descartes — and all those after him — substitute their cold, abstract philosophical idea of deity for the Christian heritage of a personal God who reveals himself in history and redemptively becomes incarnate in Jesus of Nazareth.

The Church which had so nurtured Descartes chose to reject his "materialistic" rationalism in favor of the "Christian reasoning" of another mathematician, Blaise Pascal (1623-1662). Where Descartes was a "Catholic philosopher" in the sense that he was a philosopher who was Catholic, Pascal was a Catholic philosopher in showing how the Christian revelation lights up the reality behind philosophy. From him, the Church learned not to place undue trust in scientific knowledge for gaining answers to the human problem, for that way ignores the multidimensional character of reality, and artlessly leads only to atheism or deism. Small wonder, for it amounts to using reason to reach the infinitely incomprehensible. And it results in the defenders of God employing ever-regressing arguments for the possibility of God's "existence" — a logical "no win" assignment.

Pascal, on the other hand, taught the world that man is incomprehensible to himself apart from divine revelation. Without revealed insight into the nature and destiny of humankind, one can know nothing of the need for redemption, or the name of the redeemer. The result of a materialist view of humanity is either the deist who knows something of God, but nothing of his own misery and need for God; or it ends up in atheism, knowing its own misery but nothing of God.

One must ask, Who would be so naïve as to fall into the "philosopher's trap" of materialist thought? In this country, the irony is that the authors of unbelief were precisely those who had been commissioned to defend the faith. Amid the nineteenth century's turbulent society-shaping movements for emancipation, truly devout Christians — advocating for an America more in tune with its founding ideals — inadvertently dissolved the revelatory content of Christian faith into the gospel of social reform. In the

---

3. *Descartes: Philosophical Writings,* selected and translated by Norman Kemp Smith (New York: Random House, 1958), pp. 118-119.

hands of often bold and creative translators of the faith, the abolitionist, progressive, and modernist movements all eventually reduced faith to its immanent and immediate relevance for improving societal conditions. And, in the process, they neglected or denied Christianity's transcendent and eternal dimension. The loss of the vertical was well under way.

A Culture without Transcendence

The century between the "progressive orthodoxy" of Horace Bushnell (1802-1876) and the "Honest to God" theology of John A. T. Robinson (1919-1983) saw a fundamental revision of Christianity take place within liberal Protestantism. Slowly, but surely, mainline Protestant thought slid ever downward from a Christian faith anchored in the great tradition of the ecumenical creeds to a social gospel only tenuously tied to anything re-sembling orthodox faith: from a strict Trinitarian to a more nearly Unitar-ian belief; from a supernatural belief rooted in revelation to a theological naturalism reliant upon reason and science; and from a faith focused upon God's reconciling deed in Christ to a flaccid optimism about the perfect-ibility of man and society. Thus, American Protestantism has ended up with a humanized God, a God of manageable proportions quite consistent with Descartes' premises about what can be known as true. Essentially, a new religion had taken the place of the traditional Christianity of Pascal: a belief in goodness, not in God; a devotion to duty, not to a divine Lord; a church of good intentions, not a worshipping community enrapt in the ad-oration of a transcendent deity.

And America was left with a culture whose basic assumptions about reality have been drained of the supernatural. One example of the way as-sumptions have changed is the current state of the term "believer." Neuhaus makes the point that today this word, once a designation of re-spect, commonly is taken to denote a liability: that is, it refers to someone governed not by facts but by feelings and values. A believer is thought to be a victim of intellectual vacuity, a person trapped in the world of pious dreams and imagination, the "subjective" realm. Meanwhile the skeptic — who places her bets on a self-contained world, devoid of intelligent design or of miracles unexplained by natural causes — is seen as steering a safe course in the realm of knowledge, facts, and reason, what is referred to as the "objective realm." Therefore, the "scientific-minded" person is accorded the advantage over the "believer" in arguments about the public good, because the former deals with hard-nosed reality, the latter with pious dreams and wishes. Obviously, if you buy this construal of secularism versus religion believers should not be granted an equal position in the debate over the social goods of our society. Thus has an anti-religious bias "won the day" by transporting an alternative secularist account of reality into the realms once occupied by a near universal Christian consensus.

The practical result is a society where the person arguing for the infinite value of human life, especially life at either extreme of helplessness — in the womb or in old age — is placed in an untenably disadvantaged position. The religiously based argument is discredited for claiming either a universal moral code or a religious conviction as a warrant for opposing a utilitarian estimate of the worth of human existence. The same is true for arguments on just war, the morality of a free market economy, objections to a Darwinist interpretation of human significance, questioning the wisdom of genetic engineering, expressing doubts about sex education in public schools, and so on ad infinitum. And it all stems from a post-Enlightenment form of atheistic materialism which prejudices our talk of God.

Now we have arrived at the real nub in today's culture wars as they have infected the Church herself, and especially her clergy. There is a spirited contest between those who value the vertical dimension in religious commitment and those who substitute the horizontal in its place. Anyone who gives priority to a relationship with God, who allows an awareness of the reality and power of human sin to temper or alter his vision for society, and who confesses a universal need for divine sacrificial atonement is suspected of being insufficiently committed to humanity's welfare. It has to do with exclusives: either you are zealously committed to the view that human behavior and happiness are rooted in material conditions, or you share the Christian vision of man as trapped in a spiritual sickness requiring divine intervention. Secularists are convinced that only the former understanding can empower you to try to solve the world's ills. From this obviously horizontal perspective, issues of social justice and equity trump concerns about a closer spiritual communion with God. The presence of one, so the argument runs, rules out the presence of the other.

Obviously, the consequences for faith are devastating. It leaves the person whose commitment to social justice is dependent on a unified worldview rooted in historic Christianity without a leg to stand on: her orienting faith is accorded competence only in the severely restricted realm of feelings and sentiment. We are left with religion as a useful fiction for someone grieving another's death, or suffering illness or the misfortunes of fate. But when the "hard" topics of the commonweal are involved — issues of economic policy, political goals, or social justice — then this private faith is ruled out of place and will not be tolerated. This bodes ill for both Church and society.

Festschrift: A Call to Faithfulness

These are strange times, indeed, when secularists attack religion with fervent devotion and professional religionists meekly adopt a new salvationist faith based on a secularized version of the gospel! To make sense of this, one must understand that the mainline churches are governed today by leaders who, by and large, take their cues from the surrounding culture rather than from their own religious traditions. Following in the footsteps of the social gospel adherents of a century ago, but — unlike them — accepting a materialist view of society, they have adopted from academia a Marxist/liberationist understanding of humanity and culture, one in which the material plays a critical role. In the process, they have lost — or bartered away — their vision of a transcendent realm. Ironically, the very element which could ground society's passions, ethically, emotionally, and heuristically — the Judeo-Christian inheritance of a vertical dimension to reality, faith's own divinely revealed view of the world — has been sold by Christian leaders for a real mess of cultural potage.

Within the national Church bureaucracies this vertical dimension now is treated as "dross" to be cleansed from the Christian heritage, out of the mistaken judgment that transcendence has been proved "scientifically false." So it is that a treasure which might have given transcendent impetus to moral and social reform has been lost. And a perspective which could have prevented penultimate concerns from becoming idolatrous has been removed, to the detriment of society and the peril of faith. It has been the role of neo-orthodox thinkers within the Christian faith to stand in opposition to this toxic brew of cultural decay and churchly apostasy.

Robert Benne, Professor Emeritus at Roanoke College, has been in the forefront of those addressing this crisis within both Church and culture. Benne is an avid practitioner in the dangerous sport called "public theology." In his hands, public theology becomes a form of Christian apologetics which takes seriously the public intelligibility of Christian dogma, even in the face of the most secular of audiences, and strives to enter into dialogue with those disputing religion's right to have a voice in the public square. Having a pedigree extending from the apostle Paul (addressing pagans on the Areopagus) to St. Augustine (disputing the libel of Christian responsibility for the fall of Rome) to C. S. Lewis *(Mere Christianity)* to Richard Neuhaus *(The Naked Public Square)*, this form of Christian argument takes seriously the public reasonableness of Christian dogma and its claims, and trusts implicitly Christianity's capacity to handle dispute within the context of critical rationality. It is this public nature of Christian theology which Benne ventures to advance in his teaching, writing, and speeches, an essential enterprise for a Church concerned with addressing current social realities.

But Benne's motive for recapturing the vitality and potency of Christian orthodoxy is born of more than concern for society. He, like Cardinal Newman, understands dogma to be the ineradicable principle of religion.[4] That is, beliefs matter. They determine the kind of people we are and the sort of society we want and the kind of God we worship. And, assuming the traditionalist understanding of truth as "by its nature universal and permanent,"[5] then beliefs are of crucial importance to the community of faith. Just so, Benne is convinced that Christianity might survive for a while with diluted or neglected dogma, but without a reformation driving the Church back to her roots, she eventually will lose spiritual, ethical, and emotional energy and die of entropy. The clear implication is that theology can never be solely the private preserve of the professional theologians, but "the priesthood of all believers" demands each ordinary Christian to think coherently about the faith and to act from basic principles derived from theological understanding. How in the world did Benne reach this conclusion?

The Formation of a Vocation

Robert Benne's theological career had its nascent stirrings in the basement of a modest Lutheran church in West Point, Nebraska, where children's

4. John Henry Cardinal Newman, *Apologia Pro Vita Sua* (New York, London, Toronto, etc.: Doubleday, Image Books, 1956, 1989), p. 163.

5. Avery Cardinal Dulles, "The Orthodox Imperative," *First Things* 165 (August/September 2006): 31-35. This essay is an incredibly convincing argument against theological relativism.

voices competed with the wheezing of exposed overhead water pipes as gospel songs wafted through the catacomb-like corridors of an old-time church. It might have lacked some of the grandeur of St. Peter's in Rome or the cathedral at Chartres, but it was home: "We preschoolers wailed when we were 'promoted' from our comfortable little room in which Jesus' disputation with the elders peered down on us from among the steam pipes."[6] The account of this accomplished theologian/ethicist/public intellectual's burgeoning consciousness of the miracle of baptismal regeneration weaves a narrative of gradual awakening to the gospel, and of a blossoming intuition that the God of the Bible just might be calling young Bobby Benne into his service.

It is a story intermittently interrupted only by the normal adolescent diversions of sports, schoolboy pranks, a resolute aversion to anything smacking of churchly unmanliness, and a wholesome doubt that this normal kid could measure up to the lofty vision of this great Church. If all this sounds suspiciously reminiscent of Lake Wobegon, it is not because personal biography has imitated Prairie Home Companion, but an indication that Garrison Keillor truly does his homework.

"What happened to you, Bob?" was the question asked by a woman who knew there was a "shaking of the foundations" between the 1960s liberal version of theologian Bob Benne and the now sixty-year-old "neo-orthodox," hard-to-pin-down and pigeon-hole *conservative*! It's a good question. Morphing from hard-driving, sports-loving, conscience-sensitive teenager to a passionate social activist in the 1960s and then to a "post-radical" theologian-ethicist involves some major intellectual leaps. And leap Bob Benne has.

Benne's spiritual and philosophical metamorphosis has been experienced in some version by more than a few for whom intellectual honesty and fidelity to ancient truths were more important than being identified with the latest trends in the academy. The larva stage in his "neo-orthodox development" began when Benne left the security — and complacency — of mid-1950s legalistic Midwestern pietism, and drank in the heady brew of Kierkegaardian existentialism and Niebuhrian realism at Midland College. Like many students who find themselves exposed to new and exciting concepts as they step on campus for the first time, Bob Benne eagerly

---

6. Robert Benne, *Reasonable Ethics: A Christian Approach to Social, Economic, and Political Concerns* (St. Louis: Concordia Publishing House, 2005), p. 13.

adopted a more "open," more liberal Protestant view of the faith than the one he had acquired in catechetical classes.

Whatever break was involved in the questioning of once taken-for-granted certainties within the hallowed confines of this Lutheran college must have intensified many-fold as grants and fellowships led him first to far-off Erlangen, then to "far-out" University of Chicago Divinity School. At the latter setting, he sat at the feet of Gibson Winter and Alvin Pitcher, both of whom were pioneering the theological critique of American history, culture, and values — and heralding the optimistic dreams of a secular city. With their searching analyses of American society and their linking of theory and praxis, Benne found himself in possession of a new understanding of the role of the biblical prophet — hence, of the contemporary Christian — in bringing God's judgment on the many and various sins and injustices of American society.

By the time of his first teaching job, at the Rock Island campus of Lutheran School of Theology in Chicago, Bob Benne fully qualified as an enthusiastic, avant-garde lay professor of ethics with prophetic portfolio. Heady times, full of idealism and social activism, were the perfect match for this new professor now fully in sync with the "triumphant" liberal Protestantism of the day. When his gifts and promise were rewarded with a teaching post at the newly merged LSTC, full-bore radical "street theater" politics had become a routine part of the academic role — and he ate it up, at least for a while.

Eventually, however, the radical posturing of the Left began to wear thin. For Benne, the heroic virtue of being on "the right side of history" began to pale next to the more modest virtue of being truthful before God and man: truthful about means and ends when it came to promoting social revolution; truthful about the real nature of justice and its attainability in this imperfect world; and a forthrightness concerning the true state of American society and its actual achievements and failures. Even when candor meant being at odds with the liberal "template," he found that he could do no other. This also meant not hedging about the authority and universality of the Christian faith. Here was the decisive issue.

Following a neighborhood rally, Benne experienced an "Augustinian garden moment" over his revolutionary certainties when one of his students turned the radical rhetoric of a "raised consciousness" against the very institutions of the Church which had nurtured this budding revolutionary. Immediately, Benne's evolving discomfort with the Left's tenden-

tious attitudes and prescriptions burst into a full-blown cognitive dissonance. Something seemed radically wrong. Maybe it was the absence of a
Niebuhrian realism in this bold new prophetic consciousness. Or maybe it
was the lack of good, old-fashioned Augustinian/Lutheran insight into
original sin and the limits of humanity's goodness that brought an end to
his flirtation with mainstream Protestantism and leftist politics. Or it
might just have been the "rebel" in Bob Benne once again refusing to be
whisked along on the tide of popular liberal Protestant sentiment.

Whatever the trigger, he lost his ability to believe in the new religion of
leftist politics which was overtaking the denominational hierarchies and
their seminaries. His solid orthodox Lutheran upbringing made it impossible to affirm a neo-pagan belief-system that had transformed the myth of
American innocent progress into the myth of American guilty regress.
Reaching this point was largely due to an awareness that the abiding Christian substance which once had determined the Protestant mainstream now
had morphed into little more than a transient enthusiasm for the weird:
"Because [the Protestant establishment] had been complicitous in this op-
pressive American history, it now had to dissociate itself from this history
of oppression and aim at transforming America from new sources that had
not been contaminated by its own dominant past. It looked to Marxism,
feminism, ecologism, multiculturalism — 'voices from the periphery' — to
purge and restore its transformist vision."[7]

A Pattern of Development: Benne's Writings

The trajectory of Benne's philosophical/theological development can be
traced in his writings. They show a gradual shift from youthful prophetic
critic of the American experiment to a more considered, more nuanced
and balanced theologian/ethicist whose grounding in Christian tradition
informed his critique of society, not vice versa. To envision this transformation, it is almost enough to know just the titles of his books in these dynamic years. *Wandering in the Wilderness: Christians and the New Culture*
(1972)[8] and *Defining America: A Christian Critique of the American Dream*

7. Benne, *Reasonable Ethics*, pp. 24-25.
8. Robert Benne, *Wandering in the Wilderness: Christians and the New Culture* (Philadelphia: Fortress Press, 1972).

14

(1974)[9] were far more sympathetic with the prevailing winds blowing through the mainline churches of the day. In the latter volume, two young theologians are trying to come to grips with the issue forced upon them by the decade 1964-1974: as believers in Christ, "How can we be Americans with integrity?"[10] Phil Hefner and he found a combination Christian theology and Sioux insight to provide an agenda for the spiritual and social regeneration of American society. These were heady days and both men were fully caught up in them.

If this early Benne was a bit too sanguine about the possibility of a new civil religion binding Americans together, his next major work more than made up for it. It was in *The Ethic of Democratic Capitalism: A Moral Reassessment* (1981)[11] that Benne sinned against the liberal establishment by revealing a scholar unwilling to submerge truth to the prevailing politically correct vision of the world. Standing as a lone contrarian to the prevailing intellectual opinion of the day, he refused to join in the "booming prophetic peals against that society and stirring calls for radical change."[12] Instead, he committed progressive academic heresy by suggesting that democratic capitalism might not be the invention of the devil. To those who reflexively denounce free market economics as the tool of the oppressors and the principle of evil in post-industrial history, this professor of ethics offered a disturbing possibility: they might be wrong. That was enough to garner him the suspicion and sometimes the disdain of many former friends.

At a minimum, there is something symbolic in Benne packing up his family and moving from bustling Chicago to Roanoke College in quaint little Salem, Virginia, not long after the publication of *Democratic Capitalism*. The loss of former allies and colleagues in the good fight to bring a Christian ethos to bear upon American society; the upheaval of changing from a restless cosmopolitan world-center to a quieter, more nearly pastoral setting; the move from a rather heterodox Lutheran seminary to a small liberal arts college open to recapturing its confessional identity — all this was involved as he made the most consequential decision of his vocation yet: establishing a Center for Religion and Society in an academic setting

9. Robert Benne and Philip Hefner, *Defining America: A Christian Critique of the American Dream* (Philadelphia: Fortress Press, 1974).

10. Benne and Hefner, *Defining America*, p. vi.

11. Robert Benne, *The Ethic of Democratic Capitalism: A Moral Reassessment* (Philadelphia: Fortress Press, 1981).

12. Benne, *Ethic of Democratic Capitalism*, p. vii.

where genuinely free intellectual inquiry were encouraged and supported, while finding his groove as wise and trusted mentor for students. The transition from radical prophet of social change to orthodox teacher of Lutheran confessional identity was well underway.

Benne's next two books have proved his credentials as one of Christianity's major ethicists of this generation and they offer for posterity some of the most coherent and practical ethical guidance, along with supporting theoretical framework, Lutherans in this country have produced. These two books not only help the struggling Christian close the gap between Sunday morning worship and the quotidian demands of daily life, but they provide a theological and philosophical grounding for those searching for a way to relate the Christian worldview, complete with its commitment to a transcendent order revealed in the scriptures, to the debates of the public square.

The former work, *Ordinary Saints,*[13] is quite literally an ethical catechism for persons needing an answer to the question of why one should travel the Christian path rather than some other, and contains wisdom far surpassing the typical college textbook on the subject. The second work, *The Paradoxical Vision,*[14] reminds Lutherans of the priceless treasure which God has entrusted to them for the sake of the whole Church of God; a treasure that is ever renewing and correcting the Christian tradition from within.

Responding to his students' patent need for a foundational understanding of the Christian/Lutheran ethos, one that was straightforward, clear, and digestible by young people in the throes of early adulthood's craziness, Bob Benne has penned one of Christianity's finest catechetical and devotional treasures. *Ordinary Saints: An Introduction to the Christian Life* (1988 & 2003) is a repository of Christian information and wisdom suitable for classroom, bedside drawer, and reference shelf. It offers college youth an intelligible brief for Christian belief and practice, giving reasons for incorporating a Christian worldview into their own, and prodding critical reflection on this culture's radical individualism. It provides adult catechumens with a mature and practical insight into the profundities of Christian dogma, from the Trinity to original sin to the truth about the moral ambiguity of much human acting and deciding. And for an age desperately in

---

13. Robert Benne, *Ordinary Saints: An Introduction to the Christian Life* (Minneapolis: Fortress Press, 1988).

14. Robert Benne, *The Paradoxical Vision: A Public Theology for the Twenty-first Century* (Minneapolis: Fortress Press, 1995).

need of an "organizing paradigm" for life in this chaotic world, *Ordinary Saints* suggests a workable vision of life from the vantage point of belief. This book is a must for pastors and professors and all Christians who work in the helping professions and who assign texts for their students.

Bob Benne's enduring theological contribution to subsequent generations is evident in his 1995 work, *The Paradoxical Vision: A Public Theology for the Twenty-first Century.* It is here we find the beating heart and the sharp criterion of his theological program; and it is where we uncover the motivating force behind his forty years of educating the young and debating the apostate. In this Lutheran primer on "what matters most" he explains the scope of an authentically public theology: "At its most profound, a religious tradition does not point to itself, but rather to the final reality that it believes is disclosed in its tradition, and it enlists millions in its vision over the stretch of hundreds, if not thousands, of years."[15] Already, the vertical dimension to Christian faith is apparent. In the Christian tradition we are dealing with a God who is distinguishable from his creation, whose being is "the infinite qualitative difference between God and ourselves" (Kierkegaard). This ontological difference brings with it an epistemological implication: God is incomprehensible apart from his revelation.

From this starting point a public theology must be faithful to two opposite poles. First, to have any legitimacy, it must be faithful to a concrete religious tradition, in Christianity's case to a vertical dimension which cannot be compromised. It cannot adapt itself to the culture to the extent that it becomes, in effect, a perversion of the revealed faith it represents. Second, there is a practical engagement with its cultural context which leads to the tradition interpreting and trying to persuade that environment with credible argument.

Benne is convinced that the Lutheran tradition is not, as some see it, a historically conditioned albatross around the neck of anyone trying to influence American culture. Instead, it is a precious non-sectarian resource from the broad catholic tradition, one too often neglected. Many intellectuals have bemoaned the weighty heritage of Lutheran confessional identity, seeing it as baggage to be discarded so that Christian faith might be found relevant to contemporary American life. Not Benne; he is convinced the critics have delved too shallowly into the Lutheran genius. Consequently, they have missed the most salient point: Christianity does not

---

15. Benne, *The Paradoxical Vision*, p. 5.

prove its truth by being relevant, but by conforming to the interpretation of our lives given by God in the gospel.

The most nearly apt term for capturing the key Lutheran insight for public theology, says Benne, is "paradox." This foundational concept, "crucially present in the biblical and Christian tradition generally, [is] neglected at the peril of authentic Christian teaching and practice."[16] The defining paradox, of course, is the crucified God, Jesus Christ: "in the unique and specific event of Jesus as the Christ — his ministry, death, and resurrection — the lost world in its entirety and for all time has been retrieved by a loving God."[17] This is sheer foolishness in the eyes of the world, but for those with eyes opened by divine grace it is the wisdom of God and the power of God. This is paradox in its purest form.

Within astute Lutheran theological circles, "paradox" carries the faint echo of Luther at Heidelberg using paradox to defend grace against the encroachments of law, or of the great reformer wielding the same rhetorical weapon in his battle against Erasmus over the specious notion of a "freedom of the will." For our life in the world, the crucial paradox is that we unworthy sinners are, by grace, justified before the courts of God while we are yet sinners. Paradox resides at the innermost heart of the Christian faith.

Used in political reasoning, the concept of paradox serves to keep in focus the central themes governing a Christian worldview, and without which the public discourse would not only be stripped of an ancient and venerable linguistic heritage, but would be radically impoverished of crucial philosophical insight into man and his worldly structures. In the American context, political argumentation devoid of Christian foundational ideas about man's dual nature too easily undercuts the Founders' preference for stability over social engineering, division of powers over efficiency, and limited government over radical notions of equality. Paradox is central to the idea of human nature embodied in the founding documents of the American experiment.

So, for example, political thinkers imbued with a paradoxical perspective bring a dual view of the nature of humanity. "Humans are an inextricable mixture of nature and spirit."[18] Man does not live by bread alone; but neither is he some disembodied angel capable of surviving on ether. There

---

16. Benne, *The Paradoxical Vision*, p. 68.
17. Benne, *The Paradoxical Vision*, p. 64.
18. Benne, *The Ethic of Democratic Capitalism*, p. 27.

is a damnably stubborn complexity about the human species, and all attempts to gloss over or deny this fundamental reality by seeing him as "commercial creature" or "material being" must be viewed as, a priori, unrealistic and dangerous. Religiously, this aptly fits the Christian view of man as freighted with original sin. Christianity views humanity as *simul justus et peccator*, at the same moment fully justified and imputed "good" before God; and yet he is simultaneously sinful, egoistic, guilty, and incapable of the truly good which the neighbor needs and which God requires. The human predicament is that man unfailingly is a disappointment to himself and others because he is ensnared in "what Augustinians describe as *libido dominandi*."[19] He is trapped in self-assertion. Seen from the vantage point of the paradoxical, human ambiguity and the dilemma of human striving are the primary truths about man. Once the paradoxical slant becomes seated in a political theorist's outlook, she will be wary of all speculation that fails to take into account this problematic view of humanity.

Obviously, the implications for society are profound. It means that the Marxist and liberal interpretation of man's plight suffers from a shallow estimate of man: "the fundamental cause of human egoism is not in the external conditions of society — private property or the relations of production — but inherent in the internal conditions of human nature itself."[20] Granted human self-seeking is the toxin of individual striving, even more destructive and ineradicable is the "will-to-power" of group life. This is what makes so lethal the humanist infatuation with socialism, not to mention Marxism. "Humanist readers swallow Marxist and socialist economic interpretations for their moral appeal, not for their empirical validity."[21] Without a vision of the absurdity and inconsistency of the human, no safeguard against this inclination toward corporate self-aggrandizement is possible.

From this key Christian insight flows faith's infamous modesty: a "Lutheranized" political theorist or actor will not easily be seduced into grandiose proposals for "making the U.S. budget in line with Jesus' sermon

---

19. Charles T. Mathewes, *Evil and the Augustinian Tradition* (Cambridge: Cambridge University Press, 2001), p. 46. Also, I am indebted to Jean Bethke Elshtain for alerting me to the reigning idea in our culture that everything can be negotiated and there is no need for violence in our reasonable world. It is further evidence of the loss of Christian insight in the public arena. See Jean Bethke Elshtain, *Just War against Terror: The Burden of American Power in a Violent World* (New York: Basic Books, Perseus Books Group, 2003).

20. Benne, *The Ethic of Democratic Capitalism*, p. 33.

21. Benne, *The Ethic of Democratic Capitalism*, p. 12.

on the mount" (a Lutheran bishop advocates this!); nor will a politician fall prey to grand designs for wiping out poverty in our time (a U.N. goal); nor will the layman be so gullible as to cooperate in a plot to change the definition of biblical morality (by "adopting" homosexuality as a normal human activity.) Rather, the individual chastened by insight into the paradoxical nature of the "righteous soul" will argue that God works his providential care through both state and Church (the two-fold rule of God), through both law and gospel (excluding both theocracy and Erastianism), through both reason and faith. The paradoxical vision keeps in the forefront a view of humanity and its projects that is infinitely respectful, but perpetually wary.

This means faith can never, in this world, be replaced by sight or understanding. There are unbridgeable limits to human understanding, this side of the eschaton, which are way too profound to permit seeking "the best" at the expense of "the good." Utopian schemes to build a perfect world ought to be immediately suspect to a Christian drenched in paradox. Despite the many accomplishments of Christian crusades in this country — all of them movements lacking a paradoxical perspective — they have contributed to a dominant ethos of "triumphalism" that seeks to push beyond faith's borders in order to erect God's kingdom on earth, come hell or high water. The typical outcome of such messianic pretensions is a state pretending to do the Church's work and a Church failing to do her central mission.

Chastened by the paradoxical vision, the orthodox Christian can hope more modestly, act more humbly, and propose more charitably: "Christian faith denies any salvific power in the policies of government. The state is to seek order and justice, but it can never save our souls before God. It has the task of seeking penultimate goods. It will be fortunate to achieve a modicum of justice in this turbulent world."[22]

More importantly, the gospel itself is at stake in maintaining integrity with the paradoxical vision. Utopian dreams not only end up "sacralizing" the temporal order, thereby falling prey to idolatry, but they typically lead the reformer into apostasy from the faith: "The paradoxical vision, however, aims at cutting off such claims for even more profound reasons than their lack of empirical validity. It does so for the sake of the gospel, for its radicality and universality. The radicality of the gospel insists that salva-

22. Benne, *Ordinary Saints*, p. 193.

tion is pure gift; we do not earn it. If we do not recognize that, we dishonor God who gave his Son in this unique and decisive saving act."[23] Any alleged salvation of the world which comes at the expense of the gospel of Jesus Christ is not worth it.

By calling the Church back to this fundamental biblical insight of divine-human paradox, Benne reintroduces pastors, bishops, and "ordinary saints" to a viable stance toward the world that has been neglected of late, one crucial for recovering a public theology free of cultural domination. Paradox is the key to assuming a posture of being in the world, but not of the world. It opens the way for normative Christian concepts — law, gospel, the two-fold rule of God, the penultimate nature of all earthly dreams and designs — which can free the political thinker from the dead-end either/or alternatives of utopian scheming. Thus, Benne has made it possible to recapture treasures out of the Christian tradition which have been sadly forgotten, but which have spawned the modern world, then grown out of favor.

It has been said that the conservative stands athwart history yelling "Stop!" Always this is in response to the destructive dismantling of society. For Benne, becoming open to "conservatism" was not due to a reactionary opposition to all social change or a fearful clinging to childhood securities, but the result of a reawakening to the power and vibrancy of timeless truths of the faith. And it was motivated by the desire to be obedient to God's call upon him as teacher and apologist for the Christian treasure. Keeping faith, first with God's revealed truth, second with the culture's questions, has been his quest.

Postscript

This book is dedicated to the task of addressing the extreme challenge presented to the Church by a militant secularism inside and outside ecclesiastical circles which has led an assault on transcendence. Designed as a tribute to Robert Benne's forty years of teaching and writing as a public intellectual, it seeks to advance the discussion of Christianity's pertinence to the public square and to refine Christianity's response to the attack on religion by contemporary doubt. It is fitting that Bob Benne's career mir-

---

23. Benne, *The Paradoxical Vision*, pp. 70-71.

rors the growth of the neo-orthodox movement in Christianity, with its retrieval of the Church's true heritage and of religion's proper role in the marketplace of ideas.

Despite glaring differences in their formal ecclesiologies and in their personalities, there is a striking affinity between Bob Benne — the man and the teacher — and the nineteenth-century prophetic scold, Søren Kierkegaard. Both have little tolerance for those who take lightly the fearsome responsibility of handling faithfully the received heritage of God's word. Both hate sham and hypocrisy. Both were placed by God in a Church gone astray, and needing the corrective of faith's perspective. And both saw the Church's apostasy in the same light: "If the human race had risen in rebellion against God and cast Christianity off from it or away from it, it would not have been nearly so dangerous as this knavishness of doing away with Christianity by a false way of spreading it."[24] This book, like Benne, seeks to address the knavishness of our day.

---

24. Søren Kierkegaard, *Attack upon "Christendom": 1854-1855*, trans. Walter Lowrie (Princeton: Princeton University Press, 1944), p. 35.

The Crux of Christianity's Case:
The Resurrection of Jesus

Carl E. Braaten

Twentieth-century biblical scholarship was pretty much unanimous in the discovery that the New Testament from beginning to end was written from the perspective of belief in the resurrection of Jesus of Nazareth. The entire motive for remembering Jesus and writing down the accounts of his life and teachings, decades after he was crucified, was the belief of his closest friends and followers that he was alive and present and anything but dead and gone. But among contemporary theologians and biblical scholars there is no consensus that Jesus really did rise from the dead, or that the resurrection remains an essential belief of the Christian faith today. To the question, "Can we still be Christians today without believing in the reality of Jesus' resurrection?" some theologians said "yes," and some said "no." The result has been a huge controversy, one that has spilled beyond academic debate into the life of the churches, reflected in what is preached from the pulpits and believed in the pews.

In this essay I will try to show what difference it makes whether we believe or disbelieve that God raised Jesus from the dead. Notoriously, some professors are teaching in our seminaries that the resurrection is a dispensable belief, and that we can be good Christians without holding fast in faith to the creedal affirmation of the resurrection of Jesus. Well, I don't believe that. In the fourth century the great controversy in the church was between trinitarian and unitarian theology. Was God one being in three persons, or was God a singular monad without any inherent personal distinctions? In the fifth century theologians were contesting whether Jesus was the divine Son of God or merely an exceptional human being. And the church said, he is both divine and human. In the sixteenth century the raging debate was whether salvation occurs solely by God's gift of grace received through faith alone, or whether we poor sinners are required to perform enough good works to merit salvation. In this century the great controversy is which God to believe in, in a world of many religions and many putative deities. If we believe in the God of the early Christians, then we believe in the living God who raised Jesus from the dead. In the resurrection God identified himself with the cause of Jesus. From that point on, when we think of God, we think of Jesus, and when we think of Jesus we think of God. Henceforth, we cannot think of one without the other. The Nicene Creed coined some phrases to make this linkage stick: Speaking of Jesus, it says: ". . . God from God . . . true God from true God . . . of one Being with the Father." We believe in God who "gives life to the dead and calls into existence the things that do not exist," for Jesus' sake. And I can see Luther slamming his fist down on the pulpit, shouting the words, *"Und es gibt kein andrer Gott."* There is no other God, no other God than the one who raised Jesus from the dead. So, that is our first important point, something that goes to the heart of the Christian faith, surely as much as belief in the Triune God or the divinity of Christ. The resurrection tells us who God is and which God is the true God among all the gods and idols in the universe of religions. Without faith in the resurrection of Jesus — let there be no mistake about it — Christianity will have morphed into a different religion.

Now I believe we should acknowledge in all humility that we have no theory to explain the resurrection. Here modesty is the better part of wisdom. We have no theory and we need no theory to explain the resurrection of Jesus. It would be silly to hold that an explanation is needed in order to receive the benefits of resurrection faith. That would be like refusing to watch television unless one could explain how electricity works, or like refusing to admit one had fallen in love before explaining how it happened. When the apostle Paul spoke to the Athenian philosophers in front of the Areopagus, he did not adjust his telling of the good news about Jesus and the resurrection to fit their metaphysical beliefs. If he would have done that, he would have talked about immortality, not about resurrection. In Greek or Hellenistic metaphysics there could be no such thing as a resurrection. It just couldn't happen. Why? Because the Greeks believed in the immortality of the soul; Jews believed in the resurrection of the body. Paul was a Jew. He told the Greeks something new, and to them it probably sounded like babbling nonsense. God will judge the world by Jesus, and this he guaranteed by raising him from the dead. Some scoffed, but some believed. Same old story, now as then. The only difference is that nowadays many of the scoffers are to be found inside the churches, among bishops, seminary professors, and parish pastors. I can imagine Paul commenting, "What a pitiful thing, what a bunch of fools to imagine that we can still be Christian without a resurrection faith."

The second critical emphasis I would make is that the resurrection of Jesus is an *eschatological event*. The first witnesses who claimed to have seen Jesus alive after his crucifixion did not use the word "eschatological." It is a heavy theological term that refers to a whole nexus of things the early Christians did believe in. They got it from Jesus and Jesus got it from the Rabbis who taught him the Hebrew faith. The central idea in eschatology is the kingdom of God. The kingdom of God that Jesus proclaimed was the oncoming power of God, inaugurating the reign of peace, righteousness, and justice, and putting an end to suffering, violence, and poverty. The Beatitudes are the best expression of this idea. Such a world we can only hope for; it does not now exist, and it cannot exist under the present conditions of life, under the tyranny of sin, death, and the power of the devil. Eschatology means that there is hope for a fundamental transformation of the conditions of life we now know, beckoning a new future of life beyond the certainty of death. In the end such a future can only be brought about by God. It cannot happen gradually by cosmic or natural evolution, nor suddenly by social or political revolution. It can only be brought about by a miraculous apocalyptic intervention of God.

"Apocalyptic" is a technical theological word that has little in common with its general Hollywood usage. It literally means "revelation." The last book of the Bible is named "The Apocalypse," because it is a revelation of the end-times, dealing with the last things and the final future of the world. The resurrection of Jesus can only be understood within the framework of Jewish apocalyptic eschatology. Put more simply, the resurrection of Jesus is the revelation of an event above and beyond the finality of death. It is the beginning of something really new. We have been given the revelation that God has raised Jesus from the dead, and that gives us sufficient reason to hope for life beyond the grave. In spite of the guillotine of death that is our inescapable universal human destiny, we have reason to hope for eternal life with God and all the saints whom God chooses by his amazing grace to recruit for his everlasting kingdom. We know we have to die, yet on account of Christ and his resurrection from the dead, we hope and trust that life will ultimately prevail over death. Humanly speaking, death is the last word. But for Christ's sake death becomes only the next to the last word, the penultimate word. The last word is the great transformation of life, an everlasting future with God and all those whom God's love embraces. Without resurrection faith we would live as people who have no hope for life beyond death, despair, and annihilation. Who can deliver a death blow to death? Who can counter the deadliness of death, if not the God of hope, the God who raised Jesus from the dead?

Many moons ago I spent a sabbatical year at Oxford University. That year Paul van Buren was invited to be a guest lecturer at the university. He had just written a book entitled, *The Secular Meaning of the Gospel*. The book was an attempt to adjust the Christian faith to the philosophy of logical positivism (e.g., A. J. Ayer and others). That was the philosophy asserting that for a statement to be true it had to be empirically verifiable. That means it would need to stand the test of what can be proved by sensory data or a laboratory experiment. Obviously, in that case most beliefs we confess in the Creed would have to go. I invited Paul van Buren to an evening of theological discussion with other American scholars also on sabbatical. We came around to the question of the resurrection of Jesus. For him it meant only the courage to die for what you believe. Like Socrates. And what about our having to die? He said, "Modern man is no longer afraid of death." I will never forget that. I thought I was a modern man, so why am I scared to death of death? Is it really true that "modern man is no longer afraid of death"? My answer at the time was, all the evidence points to the fact that modern people as much as ancient and medieval people are afraid to die, otherwise why do they spend so much time and money trying to cover it up? Why do we drown out the voice of death by the clatter of noises? Why do we try to beautify death with garlands of roses? Why do we use euphemisms like "passing on" and "going home"? Why do we use cosmetics to make dead people look like they are only sleeping? Why are poor people willing to pay for expensive funerals when a family member dies? Why are people numbing themselves with deafening music, and why are they getting high on drugs?

Resurrection hope tells us something definitive about the nature of human being. The psalmist asked, "What is man that thou art mindful of him?" Philosophers have long pondered the question of the essence of humanity, what distinguishes humans from their animal friends. Immanuel

Kant, perhaps the greatest of German philosophers, stated in his *magnum opus, The Critique of Pure Reason,* that there are three great questions that concern a rational and reflective human being: (1) "What can I know?" (2) "What ought I to do? (3) "What may I hope?" The answer to the first question has to do with science. The answer to the second question deals with ethics and morality. It is the business of religion to answer the third question.

Hope lies at the heart of human existence. Where there is life there is hope, and where there is hope, there is religion. The religion that best responds to the universal human quest for a total hope founded on truth is what we claim for Christianity. It is up to Christian theology to show — I would even like to say "prove" — that this is so, and why it is so. Here and now we can only scratch the surface. This has to do with what we call apologetics in theology. Apologetics is giving reasons for what one believes. First Peter 3:15 puts it this way: "Always be prepared to make a defense to any one who calls you to account for the hope that is in you."

Some people seem satisfied to deal only with the first two questions. They study hard and learn a lot. They pride themselves on living a decent moral life, being good to others, and practicing the Golden Rule. Their focus in life is summed up by knowledge and morality. And these are important aspects of being human. But are they enough? We believe that hope reaches down to an even deeper level. As Schleiermacher argued against rationalism in his *Speeches on Religion,* hope is not something added on to knowledge and morality. Hope is something people express in symbols and myths, legends and sagas, liturgies and songs, chronicles and stories. Not all of these present a single coherent message, but they do express the deepest longings and fears of human beings.

The utterances of hope are signals concerning the human condition. They indicate that we humans are on our way, like a ship suffering distress at sea on its path to a destination. The symbols of the different religions clash with each other as to the nature of the distress and the destination ahead. We all know that religions profoundly disagree with each other, and the proof is all the wars of religion, not only in the past but in today's world. Secular and naturalistic theories claim that there is no distress and no destination. They are shallow and superficial, and I would even say "stupid" for blinding themselves to the meaning inherent in things that concern human beings in an ultimate way, things that bear on the existential issues of life and death, to be or not to be. A religion is a ritualized system of hope that functions like an SOS signal. A person does not hope if there is nothing wrong or lacking, for it is meaningless to talk of hoping for something one already has. So hope sends a dual message, first, that something essential is lacking, and secondly, that there exists a possibility of rescue and help. The one brings into view the human limitation, and the other the possibility of overcoming it. Poets and prophets, mystics and saints are remembered because they explored the dreadful depths of the human condition from which hope seeks deliverance. So they delve into such negative aspects of the human condition as mortality, guilt, evil, fallibility, and fault. If we sit in darkness, we long for the break of day; if life is a tribulation, we long for relief; if we are stricken by illness, health is on our minds; if we are condemned to slavery, we yearn for freedom; if exiled, our thoughts turn to the homeland.

Hope points in two directions; it points to the present, whatever the state of our predicament; and it points to the future, on the lookout for something really new that will deliver us from whatever ails us, whether doubt, despair, or death. Here is where the gospel of Jesus' resurrection comes powerfully into play. The Bible reveals the God of Israel as the God of history, the God of hope, the God who is the world's future. Abraham is the father of many nations; he went on hoping, when hope seemed hopeless. Abraham lived by promise, and promise is always oriented to the future. With Moses the religion of Israel became the story of exodus from slavery and oppression. When the Israelites were wandering around in the wilderness, they looked forward in hope for the land of promise flowing with milk and honey. The whole Old Testament is a book of hope. As Israel moved forward in history, her hope got wider and wider. She hoped not only for herself, but for all the nations, and not only for the nations here and now, but for all things and the entire world. The widening of hope continued for Israel, not only for a better future *in* history on this side of death, but for a glorious future *of* history on the other side of death. There is more to hope for than milk and honey. It was precisely this widening of hope for fulfillment beyond death that gave rise to the apocalyptic vision and promise of resurrection. Hope took a major leap forward from the Old Testament to the New Testament in the story of Jesus' resurrection. The resurrection is the Christian answer to the deeply embedded question of hope and to the forward-looking quest of Israel for a fulfillment of God's promises to the patriarchs and prophets. As Paul stood before King Agrippa, he testified: "And now I stand here on trial for hope in the promise made by God to our fathers, to which our twelve tribes hope to attain, as they earnestly worship night and day. And for this hope I am accused by Jews, O king! Why is it thought incredible by any of you that God raises the dead?" (Acts 26:6-7) This is a hope based on the solid foundation of what God did in raising Jesus from the dead, a sure and certain hope.

Earlier we mentioned the sharp contrast between the Jewish-Christian hope for resurrection of the body and the Greek-Hellenistic belief in the immortality of the soul. In relation to this dichotomy American religion is more akin to the religion of the ancient Greeks. Most religious Americans profess that they believe that humans have souls and that the souls are immortal. The body dies, but not the soul. In the Bible there is no such antinomy; instead, the dominant biblical picture involves a psychosomatic unity of body and soul. They are not two forms of existence that just happen to get mixed up with each other for a brief spell on earth, and when death comes, they separate. The biblical view of personhood cannot be squared with the Greek-Hellenistic idea of salvation as salvaging the soul from its dungeon in the body. For the Hebrews, a person's soul is in his flesh, in his eyes and ears, hands and feet, liver and heart, blood and breath, in short, in all his members and senses.

We Christians believe in the resurrection of the body. God created us humans as bodily creatures. So the body is good. The Genesis story of the fall is not about an immortal soul falling into a mortal body; it is about a whole person falling into sin and alienation from God, affecting and, indeed, infecting the whole of humanity. Paul said, "So all have sinned and fall short of the glory of God" (Rom. 3:23). He also said, "So glorify God in your body" (1 Cor. 6:20). In the early church there were people bringing the Hellenistic spirit into the church — they were called gnostics. They taught that the soul is homesick because it has descended into a material body. They believed that humans must struggle to get free of their flesh and this world of matter. The orthodox fathers answered that the body is good, not evil. And there is nothing the matter with matter, because God created it, and he doesn't create junk.

The incarnation of the Son of God in a human body underscores the belief that the body is good. The body is therefore called by Paul "the temple of the Holy Spirit." The Hellenistic philosopher Plotinus confessed that he was ashamed of having a body. He remarked, "the true philosopher is entirely concerned with the soul and not the body. He would like, as far as he can, to get away from the body . . . to dissever the soul from communion of the body. . . . True philosophers despise the body."[1]

And now a bit of bad news. In spite of the triumph of Christian orthodoxy over the gnostic heresy, some of the gnostic spirit seeped into the thinking of many Christians, lay folks and clergy. I call this popular dualistic thinking about body and soul a gnostic hangover, whereby the soul is thought to be the noble part, the higher spiritual part, and the body the inferior side. When the early Christians preached the resurrection of the body in a Greek-speaking world, the message was counter-cultural, and it seemed unbelievable. Would God appear in human flesh? The Gospel of John says "yes": "The Word became flesh," the Word who was very God of very God.

Because Jesus was raised, not as an immortal soul but as a spiritual body, there are many implications that follow. Paul said, believers are united with Christ in a new body alive with the Spirit. And this makes all the difference in how they live. Anything that competes with this new orientation of the body in unity with Christ is a sin — a sickness unto death — like having sex with a prostitute, or engaging in sexual relations with a person of the same gender, or like eating meat in heathen temples. For such things make the body a partner of deeds that do not spring from the new life in Christ.

On another front, consider this: every time we come to the Table of the Lord, we hear these words, "This is my body." We partake of the body of Christ in the sacrament of eating bread and drinking wine. It is the most important thing a believer can do at least every week — Martin Luther would have said, preferably every day. Yet, modern Lutherans have become more than a little cavalier and lazy, assessing weekly communion to be sufficient. Indeed, more than a few Lutherans think that once a month is just about right. In Northfield, Minnesota, St. John's Lutheran, a congregation of which my wife and I were members, held a series of Sunday morning forums to discuss whether to go from two times a month to celebrating Holy Communion every Sunday. The pastor wanted a weekly observance, but he did not want the issue to split the congregation. In one of the forums he asked me to stand up and give my opinion. The opposition staked its argument on the proposition that if we were to partake of the

1. Quoted by D. R. G. Owen, *Body and Soul* (Philadelphia: The Westminster Press, 1956), p. 39.

eucharist every Sunday, the Lord's Supper would become routine and boring, something one just takes for granted. So when I rose to my feet to address the issue, I asked a series of rhetorical questions: Should I give up having breakfast every morning because it is so routine? Should I give up brushing my teeth three times a day because it's so boring? Should I give up sleeping with my wife every night, because it might become something we just take for granted? But, more importantly, consider this: there were no Christians in the early centuries who gathered for worship on the Lord's Day without communing with Christ and with each other in sharing the meal of bread and wine. A lady stood up in a row behind me, after I sat down, quite beside herself and quivering with anger. She said, "All right, if we do it every Sunday, then you come and wash the communion cups. It's a lot of work." The congregation now celebrates the eucharist every Lord's Day. What is at stake in such a decision is whether or not we take seriously the greatest miracle that has ever happened, the resurrection of Jesus from the dead. Here is the most eloquent way, almost the only way, we can proclaim the death and resurrection of Jesus until he returns in glory. Eating and drinking are bodily events, and they are the most spiritual transactions in a believer's life and in the common life of a whole people.

With regard to ethics, belief in the resurrection of the body has everything to do with our political choices. We have dealt a bit with sex and liturgy, and now a word about politics. Is there such a thing as resurrection politics? In the early Corinthian church Paul accused the spiritual enthusiasts of not discerning the body. They were practicing a class distinction between the rich and the poor, between first- and second-class members in the communal body. The rich would eat first, and then the others. A negative attitude to the body leads to the breakdown of the social order. Bodily relationships have to do with food, water, shelter, clothes, and medicine, especially underscored by the one who said, "Come, O blessed of my Father, inherit the kingdom prepared for you from the foundation of the world; for I was hungry and you gave me food, I was thirsty and you gave me drink, I was a stranger and you welcomed me, I was naked and you clothed me, I was sick and you visited me, I was in prison and you came to me" (Matt. 25:34-36). The seed of this concern for justice and mercy is respect for the body.

In conclusion we will summarize what we have been asserting: We maintain that the resurrection of Jesus is the ground of the Christian belief in the resurrection of the body, in contrast to the gnostic belief in the immortality of the soul. Jesus was raised a spiritual body, a *soma pneumatikos*. This means the resurrection was not an event of Jesus coming back to life, like Lazarus. Lazarus was raised from the dead, but he had to die again. Jesus ascended into heaven in a spiritual body, never to have to die again.

Although our resurrection belief is an object of faith, it is not an arbitrary belief without reason. The English New Testament theologian, N. T. Wright, says that although the resurrection is not something we can prove by historical scholarship, yet the best historical explanation we have for the birth of the Christian church is that Jesus really did rise from the dead. Faith opens the eyes of reason. It is not irrational to believe in the resurrection of Jesus.

We have also affirmed that true Christianity stands or falls with belief in the resurrection. David Griffin, a process theologian, offers his opinion that belief in the resurrection of Jesus is purely optional. He writes: "Christian faith is possible apart from belief in Jesus' resurrection in particular and life beyond bodily death in general."[2] To the contrary, we maintain that the resurrection is a defining belief, that Christianity without the resurrection is a different religion.

The resurrection of Jesus defines who God is. God is the one who raised Jesus from the dead. If we let go of the God who gives life to the dead, we will meet only the God of wrath and we will be left in our sins. Lutherans like to say that the doctrine of justification by faith is the article by which the church stands or falls. That was Luther's stand against Rome in the sixteenth century. But at that time there were few who doubted the resurrection. The article of justification would be groundless without the prior belief in the resurrection. It's the death and resurrection of Jesus that puts money in the bank that God spends in declaring sinners to be righteous.

The incarnation and the resurrection of Jesus brought about a revolution in the definition of being human, because the body becomes an essential dimension of the human being. Souls don't walk around and say, we are somebody. Souls don't get married and have babies. Souls don't eat and drink at the Lord's Table. Souls don't vote. We believe in the resurrection of the body, and not the immortality of the soul. Deeply embedded in the human heart is the longing for life beyond death. As Christians we believe God will raise us up as spiritual bodies to live in everlasting communion with Jesus and all the saints.

---

2. David Griffin, *A Process Christology* (Philadelphia: Westminster Press, 1973), p. 12.

Without belief in the resurrection of Jesus the Christian church would never have been born. There would have been no mission to the Gentiles. Some years ago an orthodox Jew wrote a book on the resurrection. The author's name was Pinchas Lapide. The title of his book is *The Resurrection of Jesus: A Jewish Perspective*. It is a marvelous little book. His thesis is shocking. After a critical examination of all the documentary evidences, he concludes in favor of the historical facticity of the resurrection of Jesus. He says, Jesus really did rise from the dead. In his own words, he says, "I accept the resurrection of Easter Sunday not as an invention of the community of disciples, but as a historical event."[3] But then comes the twist: that does not prove Jesus is the Messiah that all believing Jews were expecting. Jesus really did rise from the dead, yes, but does that prove he is the Messiah? No! Why not? Because when the Messiah comes, he will bring in the kingdom of God, and that will change the world. But, he says, look out the window, read the morning newspaper, and you'll notice that nothing has changed. The world remains the same. The Rabbis of old never tired of saying, "If it is true that the Messiah of which our ancient prophets spoke has already come, how then do you explain the present state of the world?" But Lapide understands that the resurrection of Jesus is foundational for Christians. It is a core belief. Except for faith in the resurrection of Jesus as a real historical occurrence, Christianity would never have gotten beyond Jerusalem. As Lapide put it to a Bultmannian skeptic, "You, my dear friend, would today still be offering horse meat to Wotan on the Godesberg."[4]

The Rabbis are right, the messianic kingdom that the prophets foretold has not arrived in the way they expected. The expectations had to be transformed by Jesus and his death on the cross. So, while Jews preached the kingdom of God, and Jesus, being a Rabbi, also preached the kingdom of God, the apostles preached Jesus Christ. Our only viable Christian answer to the paradoxical position of Lapide is the apostolic one: the kingdom is present but hidden in the person of the Messiah Jesus and the good news of this event can be received only through faith. Meanwhile, we live as Christians between the times. The kingdom has come in the person of Jesus, the Messiah, the bringer of the kingdom. He is the King of the king-

---

3. *Jewish Monotheism and Christian Trinitarian Doctrine*, A Dialogue by Pinchas Lapide and Jürgen Moltmann, trans. Leonard Swidler (Philadelphia: Fortress Press, 1981), p. 59.

4. Lapide and Moltmann, *Jewish Monotheism and Christian Trinitarian Doctrine*, p. 68.

dom. But the arrival of the final kingdom in all its fullness and glory to transfigure the world in a fundamental way — that has not yet happened. Thus the kingdom is split chronologically into an already and a not yet. What has already happened is only the first fruits — preliminary, provisional, proleptic. The fulfillment, the *parousia,* is still to come.

Our Easter celebration centers on the person of Jesus, on Christ the King, in spite of the fact that the kingdom of God in its fullness remains still outstanding, as long as the world is subject to so much pain and suffering, poverty and oppression, hunger and death. Without Easter we would be people without hope. Alfred Loisy, the French historian, said, "Jesus preached the kingdom of God, and what came was the church."[5] What a letdown! What a disappointment! The church doesn't look much like the kingdom of God. But from a eucharistic perspective we can say: In spite of all the failures, scandals, and shortcomings of the church down through the ages and around the world, in spite of the fact that the church is not the kingdom in its fullness, we do have the down payment of the kingdom in the body of Christ, the real presence of Christ in the Word and the Sacraments; we do have the Scriptures; we do have the memories of the saints and the martyrs who have given us their unforgettable witness to the transforming power of the Spirit in their lives, and we do have the baptismal gift of participation in the universal mission of the gospel to the ends of the earth and to the close of the age.

5. Quoted by Hans Küng, *The Church,* trans. Ray and Rosaleen Ockenden (New York: Sheed and Ward, 1967), p. 43.

A Cultural Disorder:
C. S. Lewis and the Abolition of Man

Jean Bethke Elshtain

In March 2005, the prestigious *New England Journal of Medicine* published an essay on the topic of euthanasia for newborns, printing up the "Groningen Protocol" for such procedures. *The New York Times Magazine,* July 10, 2005, reprinted those protocols under the heading "Euthanasia for Babies?" going on to ask: "Is this humane or barbaric?" This way of presenting alternatives, in the guise of neutrality, is typical of much "enlightened" opinion.

I suspect that all of us know that the average reader of *The New York Times* prefers to choose the "humane," not the "barbaric" alternative? And the humane course, of course, is the one that favors infanticide if the correct procedures are followed. Euthanasia of babies under such circumstances is the way of "reason." Those who cry "No, we must not cross that line," advance the way of "sentiment," a.k.a. un-reason.

The essayist, Jim Holt, a "frequent contributor to the magazine," asked his readers to imagine a heated dining room table argument about such matters. The way of "reason" requires "unflinching honesty." By contrast, moral "sentiments" are inertial, resisting "the force of moral reasons." The essay concludes in this way:

Just quote Verhagen's [Verhagen being the Dutch doctor who identifies himself as a pro-infant euthanasia practitioner] description of

---

This essay was written originally for oral delivery. I have knowingly worked to preserve the forthrightness and informality of a talk.

the medically induced infant deaths over which he has presided — "it's beautiful in a way. . . . It is after they die that you see them relaxed for the first time" — and even the most spirited dinner-table debate over moral progress will, for a moment, fall silent.[1]

The essayist obviously wants us to imagine the hushed atmosphere as one in which diners are overwhelmed by the vision of peace — at last — for congenitally deformed infants. I suspect that most of those in this room would fall silent from the sheer horror of it all. "Let's give these perturbed little spirits some peace at last; let's kill them."

Holt apparently believes that brutal candor about such matters is the ethically preferred route ("Yes, I'm killing them, and that's the right thing to do"), rather than the muddling through that may involve permitting multiply handicapped infants to die rather than using sustained heroic measures to keep them alive, for example. The latter is presented as "casuistic" confusion. So any course that reflects our moral uneasiness is dishonest; any course that candidly makes it easier for medical personnel to kill is honest and reasoned.

Does anyone doubt what C. S. Lewis might say about this, about the way in which healers become killers and all the rest? Those of you somewhat familiar with my work will know that these are issues that have long troubled me. I have worried in print that, in the name of "enlightenment," we are eliminating whole categories of persons. For example: so overwhelming is our animus against the less-than-perfect that nearly 90 percent of pregnancies that test positive for Down Syndrome are aborted in the United States today, all under the rubric of "choice." In the name of expanding choice and eliminating "suffering," we are narrowing our definition of humanity and, along the way, felt responsibility to create welcoming environments for all children. Indeed, the medical experts now argue that *all* pregnant women, not just those in "at risk" categories, should be

---

1. Jim Holt, "Euthanasia for Babies? Dutch doctors have proposed a procedure for infant mercy killing. Is this humane or barbaric?" *The New York Times Magazine*, 10 July 2005, pp. 11-12, 14; p. 14. Notice, too, that the euphemism "medically induced deaths" is used rather than intentional killing, a.k.a. murder. Holt also criticizes the American discussion of these matters claiming that our way of doing it is shrouded in "casuistry." This is, of course, an attack on Catholic moral theology — anytime "casuistry" is condemned you know wariness of Catholics lurks nearby — but also on the fact that Americans spend so much time discussing moral issues. For Holt this in itself seems to be a problem.

tested routinely for Down syndrome fetuses in order that they might be aborted at an earlier stage in pregnancy given more "sophisticated" tests now available.

When we aim to eliminate one version of humanity — whether through euthanasia or systematic, selective aborting of "flawed" fetuses — perhaps a suffering humanity but humanity nonetheless, we dangerously constrict the boundaries of the moral community. In his posthumously published *Ethics*, the anti-Nazi theologian Dietrich Bonhoeffer insisted that the most radical excision of the integrity and right of natural life is "arbitrary killing," the deliberate destruction of "innocent life." "The right to live is a matter of the essence, and not of any socially imposed or constructed values," Bonhoeffer proclaimed. For even "the most wretched life" is "worth living before God."[2]

As with Bonhoeffer, C. S. Lewis was writing under the shadows of Nazism and Stalinism. His essay, *The Abolition of Man*, published in 1944 and subtitled "Reflections on education with special reference to the teaching of English in the upper forms of schools," would seem at first glance to have very little to do with the grave matters with which I have begun. Not so. Lewis sees pernicious tendencies in, of all places, elementary textbooks. At first puzzling, this quickly makes sense. The general cultural milieu, a culture's *mores*, its "habits of the heart," as the great observer of the American democracy, Alexis de Tocqueville put it, are always embedded and embodied in the books we require our children to read, the books we use to teach them.

What on earth was going on with English textbooks such that C. S. Lewis would take note of them? First, he detects an embrace of subjectivism — which means, speaking epistemologically, the embrace of both positivism and emotivism. The year 1944 and the immediate post-war decades were the heyday of this approach, and it had clearly made its way into elementary schools even as it was the dominant approach to the teaching of philosophy at Great Britain's elite institutions of higher learning.

The reduction of values to subjective "feelings" — the "sentiment" opposed to "reason" of which *The New York Times* piece speaks — leads to the embrace, or is itself a fruit of the embrace, of two interlocked propositions, summarized by Lewis thus: "firstly, that all sentences containing a predicate of values are statements about the emotional state of the speaker,

---

2. Dietrich Bonhoeffer, *Ethics* (New York: Simon and Schuster, 1945), pp. 142-85.

and, secondly, that all such statements are unimportant."[3] One need not refer to the general philosophy at work "that all values are subjective and
trivial" in order to promulgate this philosophy.

Indeed, many textbook authors probably do not recognize what they
are doing to the schoolchild, suggests Lewis. Certainly the schoolchild
"cannot know what is being done to him." And in this way another "little
portion of the human heritage has been quietly taken from [school chil-
dren] before they were old enough to understand."[4]

Let me provide an illustration of this from my own experience. When
our daughter, Jenny, was in fifth grade in a progressive public school in the
town in which we then lived, one of those bucolic New England college
towns in which university students outnumbered permanent residents,
she was required to complete a work-sheet on distinguishing fact from
value — values, of course, defined as subjective opinions having no cognitive status, hence no defensible truth warrants: pure positivism. She read
aloud as she did this and as she was trying to figure things out. Her
mother, myself, got a bit agitated as I tend to do when confronted with this
sort of thing in the guise of education. To help her understand, I said,
"Well, Jenny, if I say something is 'wrong' does that mean I am stating a
fact or a value?" — values, to repeat, being the things that we all have and,
moreover, one cannot distinguish between them as they all come out of the
same subjectivist stew.

Predictably, Jenny answered that it would be a value. I continued:
"Well, Martin Luther King said slavery was wrong. Suppose there is someone who says slavery is good and we should bring it back. Couldn't we say
he is wrong and Martin Luther King is right and that slavery is bad, period?" Jenny was stumped for a moment, and troubled, and then she said:
"Well, I think slavery is wrong, too, but that is just my opinion." Our discussion didn't end there, of course, but this experience reinforces Lewis's
claim concerning the pervasiveness of the sorts of teachings he indicts in
his essay.

For Lewis, when "ordinary human feelings" are set up as "contrary to
reason" we are on dangerous ground indeed, for a botched treatment of

3. C. S. Lewis, *The Abolition of Man: or Reflections on Education with Special Reference
to the Teaching of English in the Upper Forms of Schools* (New York: Macmillan Publishing
Co., 1947, 1976), p. 15.

4. Lewis, *Abolition of Man*, p. 22.

"some basic human emotion" is not only bad literature but is moral treachery to boot. "By starving the sensibility of our pupils we only make them easier prey to the propagandist when he comes."[5] Lewis insists that in Platonic, Aristotelian, Stoic, Christian, and some Eastern religions, one finds in common "the doctrine of objective value, the belief that certain attitudes are really true, and others really false, to the kind of thing the universe is and the kind of things we are."[6] He refers to this simply as "the Tao": certain trans-cultural, universal claims.[7]

Thus, emotional states can be "reasonable or unreasonable," for one must not traffic in the false distinction between reason and emotion, rationality and sentiment. In the regnant positivism, by contrast, "the world of facts, without one trace of value, and the world of feelings, without one trace of truth or falsehood, justice or injustice, confront one another, and no *rapprochement* is possible."[8] It is all a "ghastly simplicity."[9]

Another example drawn from experience: when I was a graduate student in the late 1960s and early 1970s, this "ghastly simplicity" was the reigning epistemology. I never quite "got it," I must say, and when I tried to argue the point with my professors, having had no formal training in epistemology, it was a non-starter. It was clear that positivism was not up for debate but, rather, was assumed, taken for granted. This is no doubt one reason I wound up as a political theorist, for in a world in which a "scientific" approach allegedly dictates the severance of fact from value, political theorists and philosophers are seen as a strange breed apart who specialize in "normative claims" or "evaluation."[10] We are, in fact, regarded as rather fuzzy minded by definition. One colleague many years ago called what I and others like me do as so much "political fiction" while he trafficked in the political facts.

---

5. Lewis, *Abolition of Man*, p. 24.

6. Lewis, *Abolition of Man*, p. 29.

7. Of course, this assimilation of faith traditions is controversial but defensible in context, I would suggest. There are times when we want to clarify distinctions and differences; other times when we want to make the strongest case we can that a core or cluster of shared recognitions persists. Writing this particular essay, Lewis took the latter tack.

8. Lewis, *Abolition of Man*, pp. 30-31.

9. Lewis, *Abolition of Man*, p. 35.

10. I should note that 'real scientists' today do not work with such a simplistic severance of 'description' and 'evaluation' and other modalities of the positivistic approach. But that seems not to have made much of a dent on its practitioners in the social sciences.

For a time, I believed, overly optimistically as it turned out, that the decisive critique of positivism mounted by philosophers such as Charles Taylor and Alasdair MacIntyre, among others, had pounded the nails into the coffin of positivism in the human sciences. Not so, as it turns out. This orientation reappeared with gusto in the current regnant epistemology in the social sciences, so-called "rational choice theory."

Now is not the time to unpack rational choice, or "rat choice" as some of us prefer to call it, in any detail. Suffice to say that, expanded to become a Weltanschauung rather than utilized as a relatively modest approach to a finite series of economic decision-making processes, rat choice trivializes all statements of value: they have no truth warrant or claim; they are "externalities." Further, this economic model enshrines a reductive view of the human person as the sum total of his or her preferences, her calculations of marginal utility, for one cannot make substantive distinctions between different "utilities," between polishing one's Porsche or working in a hospice.

Within a universe limned by rat choice, everything, in principle, can be commodified. Everything, in principle, has a "price" rather than a value. Any restrictions societies draw on where human "preferences" might take us are arbitrary. There are no intrinsic goods or evils at all. Nothing is valued for its own sake. True, we may "value" babies in a certain way. This is an ancient sentiment. But it has no rational content. Instead, every "value" is reducible to a "preference" and describable in the language of maximizing utilities.[11]

Let me illustrate. Years ago, when I was teaching at a particular university, an eager candidate for a political science position gave his job talk. To him everything was a "preference." There was no other way to talk about politics or the moral life. When he had finished, I asked: "It is a curious thing, is it not? When Martin Luther King delivered his great speech, he cried, 'I have a dream', not 'I have a preference.' How do you explain this? Is there a difference?" The somewhat flustered young man indicated that what King was calling a dream was at base just another preference and so that was no different *in principle* from, say, debating marginal alterations in the price of commodities. This way of thinking surely makes a hash of our moral sentiments, of our God-given capacity to reason about that which is good, as Lewis asserts.

---

11. For an extensive critical unpacking of these issues see Jean Bethke Elshtain, *Who Are We? Critical Reflections and Hopeful Possibilities* (Grand Rapids: Eerdmans, 2000).

This, surely, is what he feared in 1944, feared that something precious and irreparable was being lost. Those debunking the normative status and truth warrants of claims of value, whether then or now, are tacitly promoting values of their own. Writes Lewis: "A great many of those who 'debunk' traditional or (as they would say) 'sentimental' values have in the background values of their own which they believe to be immune from the debunking process."[12] One thinks here of the fundamentalist skeptic who is skeptical of everything save his fundamentalism. Or the proclaimer of moral relativism who relativizes everything save his claim to moral relativism. Lewis feared this in his era; we should fear it in ours. Then and now, at least increasingly, what seems to matter is not the dignity of each and every human life but, rather, goals like "the preservation of the species" (or "maximizing reproductive capacities") in their "optimal" form — and tragically deformed or mortally ill newborns will never maximize their reproductive potential.[13] So they are without value. Too, they will never contribute to production. They would be worthless on the marketplace (so to speak), so they are without value. We might attach value to them arbitrarily, but this is emotive and not reasoned.

It is interesting, and troubling, that we are in an age of human rights *par excellence* and yet there are forces at work in our world that undermine the ontological claims of human dignity that must ground a robust regime of human rights. Some excisions of our humanity at present are obvious and in the headlines, for example, Osama bin-Laden's claim that "Americans, Jews and infidels" should be slaughtered whenever and wherever they are to be found, men, women, and children, armed or unarmed. We see the problem immediately: categories of humanity stripped of all rights rhetorically and in the actual practice of terrorists inflamed by this rhetoric.

But there are other forces at work undermining the ground of human dignity by eroding the full force of our humanity, whether whole or broken, "normal" or "abnormal," young or old. Totalizing the population biology or the econometric perspectives are two of the ways we have devised to do this. These approaches — utilitarian at base — have worked their way into medical thought and practice, including the field of "medical ethics."

I appreciate that many who share the view that seriously deformed in-

12. Lewis, *Abolition of Man*, p. 41.
13. Some critics now write of "genetic fundamentalism" to characterize the new eugenics now spreading in the West and the East.

fants should be euthanized, whether in furtherance of a particular approach or agenda or for a more generalized antipathy toward the "deformed," will no doubt be horrified by my remarks. They insist that theirs is the decent and humane solution for immeasurably difficult and painful problems. They are trying to prevent "useless suffering" — an odd locution when you think of it. What distinguishes "useless" from "useful" human suffering, as one implies the other, does it not?

Those of us working to counter the pressures at work in this matter should acknowledge these urgencies. The people one opposes are not monsters, for the most part, though there are surely some who wield the needles bearing death who are like the notorious Dr. Jack Kevorkian, "Dr. Death," with his necrophiliac obsessions and admiration of Nazi experimentation of helpless death camp inmates. Yes, the vast majority want to do the "right" thing. Lewis understood this; he understood that various ideologies, including contemporary "right to die" notions, are "arbitrarily wrenched from their context in the whole" — here his reference point is to those fundamental truths he calls "the Tao" — and "then swollen to madness in their isolation."[14] In this way, fundamental claims to human value as such are weakened, reduced to superstitions. For ". . . the Nietzschean ethic can be accepted only if we are ready to scrap traditional morals as a mere error and then to put ourselves in a position where we can find no ground for any value judgments at all."[15]

At this point in his essay, Lewis turns explicitly to "man's conquest of Nature," the way people in his era heralded a coming age of human triumph over nature's "arbitrariness." His examples of this power-over were the aeroplane, the wireless, and the contraceptive. I appreciate how hopelessly archaic such concerns sound to our contemporary ears. One has to probe deeply to make sense of it all rather than to dismiss it as the crankiness of a fuddy-duddy. Let's take contraception as an example for closer examination: the living deny existence to the not-yet-living through this method, argues Lewis, and we come to believe we can engage in "selective breeding" with "Nature as its instrument."

Harsh words, you might think. But consider. This exercise of power or, perhaps better put, the way this power is or can be exercised, implies "the power to make its descendants what it pleases" for "each new power won

14. Lewis, *Abolition of Man*, p. 56.
15. Lewis, *Abolition of Man*, p. 58.

by man is a power over man as well. Each advance leaves him weaker as well as stronger. . . . The final stage is come when Man by eugenics, by pre-natal conditioning, and by an education and propaganda based on a per-fect applied psychology, has obtained full control over himself. *Human* na-ture will be the last part of Nature to surrender to Man."[16]

Lewis held out hope that the obstinacy of "real mothers, real nurses, and (above all) real children" might preserve "the human race in such san-ity as it still possesses. But the man-moulders [sic] of the new age will be armed with the powers of an omnicompetent state and an irresistible sci-entific technique: we shall get at last a race of conditioners who really can cut out all posterity in what shape they please."[17] At the time, the reference point Lewis's readers could point to was National Socialist Germany with its cruelly enforced eugenics, and this, surely, was in Lewis's mind. I doubt many suspected that their own societies might one day enter into this dan-ger zone, not under the banner of totalitarianism but, rather, under the ru-bric of human choice and freedom. As Lewis fretted about "post-humanity," a bleak future indeed, we have our own apostles of the "post" and "transhuman" future.[18]

When C. S. Lewis in 1944 wrote of "the abolition of man," he meant the end of humanity as we know it, brought about by humanity itself and our inability to stem what St. Augustine called the *libido dominandi.* This can take such obviously disgusting and evil forms as gulags and death camps. But it can also appear in other guises and in the name of doing good. Mind you, I am not trafficking in moral equivalences here. I am not saying that contemporary "positive eugenics," as it is called, is identical to the inten-tional slaughter of millions of people because of their allegedly "under-human" *(Untermenschen)* status. But I am alerting us to the very real dan-gers in our world at the moment.

---

16. Lewis, *Abolition of Man,* pp. 71-72.

17. Lewis, *Abolition of Man,* p. 73.

18. The literature on all this is vast. The interested reader might just search for "trans-human" on the Internet and amaze — and horrify — himself or herself by the celebration of various plans and possibilities for creating a non-human future — created by human beings themselves, of course. It should also be noted that Nazi eugenics, or a version of eugenics, had infected nearly all Western societies in the 1920s and 1930s, with laws being put on the books to coercively sterilize the "unfit" and, in other ways, to prevent the "burden" on soci-ety represented by the "mentally deficient." I discuss this in detail in the book based upon my Gifford lectures, *Sovereignties: God, State, Self* (New York: Basic Books, 2008).

Current projects of self-overcoming are tricky to get at critically precisely because they are not so manifestly hideous as the horrors of the twentieth century; because they present themselves to us in the dominant language of our culture — choice, consent, control; and because they promise an escape from the human condition into a realm of near mastery. We are beguiled with the promise of a new self. Consider, then, that we are in the throes of a structure of biological obsession that undermines recognition of both the fullness and the limitations of human embodiment. A premise and promise driving the Human Genome Project was that we might one day soon intervene decisively in order to promote better if not perfect human products. Promoters of these developments ran — and run — to the ecstatic; for example, a 1986 pronouncement by a geneticist that the genome project "is the grail of human genetics . . . the ultimate answer to the commandment to 'Know thyself'."[19]

The "social imaginary" declares the human body a construction, something we make, unmake, and remake at will. We are loathe to grant the status of "givenness" to any aspect of ourselves, despite the fact that human babies are wriggling, complex, little bodies pre-programmed with all sorts of delicately calibrated reactions to the human relationships "nature" presumes will be the matrix of child nurture. If we think of bodies concretely in this way, we are then propelled to ask ourselves questions about the world little bodies enter: is it welcoming, warm, responsive? But if we tilt in the direction of genetic fundamentalism, one in which the body is raw material to be worked on or worked over, the surroundings in which bodies are situated fades as The Body gets enshrined as a kind of messianic project.

It is unsurprising, therefore, that certain experts declare as a matter of fact — the point, for them, isn't even worth arguing — that "we must inevitably start to choose our descendants." We do so now in "permitting or preventing the birth of our own children according to their medical prognosis, thus selecting the lives to come." So long as society does not cramp our freedom of action, we will stay on the road of progress and exercise sovereign choice over birth by consigning to death those with a less than stellar potential for a life not "marred by an excess of pain or disability."

What C. S. Lewis called the "extreme rationality," not to be confused with reason as such, that consigns to the dustbin of history all claims of in-

19. I go over this in detail in *Who Are We?* and in a number of essays.

trinsic value — as those embracing such truths cannot, allegedly, meet certain standards of a rationalistic defense of these values — winds up promoting a subjectivism of values it believes is somehow more honest. When this happens, those whose "values" triumph will be those possessed of the most overwhelming will-to-power. By contrast, "A dogmatic belief in objective value," Lewis writes, "is necessary to the very idea of a rule which is not tyranny or an obedience which is not slavery."[20]

We seem to have moved rather far from the real world drama of a disabled newborn being intentionally euthanized, but I hope that the reader finds this not to be the case. I hope readers see in the establishment and even celebration of deliberate infanticide as the only courageous and truly humane thing to do, as what reason not unreason dictates, the sort of thing Lewis warned us against in 1944. Why can we not love a helpless being in the time God has given her? What can this profoundly disabled newborn teach us about grace and beauty and goodness? About caritas? Why can we not ameliorate pain and discomfort without believing we must either use extraordinary measure to "keep alive" or else boldly kill?

In 2003, the eighteen-year-old son of one of my cousins died. He was "supposed" to have died when he was an infant. He was born anencephalic. He could never speak, nor feed himself, nor crawl, nor walk, nor do any of the normal things human beings generally do or learn to do. According to the doctors, there was no "there there." Aaron was definitely a prime candidate for euthanizing or, as the moral theorist Peter Singer candidly puts it (in approval), infanticide. But to anyone who met him, Aaron was a beautiful child with the biggest blue eyes and the most striking dark eyelashes imaginable. He stared out at the world, making no apparent distinctions, until his mother came into view. Then his face would "beam" or "light up" — there is no other way to put it. He knew her and he loved her

---

20. Lewis, *Abolition of Man*, pp. 84-85. This statement, with its echoes of medieval Thomism, is worth rereading several times as it runs so counter to the dogma of our time. An essayist commented recently that Lewis adhered firmly "to an objectivist account of the world. Things are as they are, however I feel about them; the world is thus, and within and throughout and beside the world is God, and his historical dealings with human beings." Whether, therefore, our own inclinations chime with Christian understanding is "quite beside the point. How I feel about the Incarnation, or the moral law, can no more affect its reality than my chafings against (say) the operations of gravity will permit me to fly unaided." See Raymond Edwards, "Fantasy Founded on Belief: Narnia Revisited," *The Tablet* 17 (14 December 2005): 22.

and I would defy anyone to claim otherwise. Her love and care and devotion kept him going for eighteen years. And when he died an entire family — parents, sibling, grandparents, aunts, uncles, cousins — and an entire community mourned their loss.

My cousin, Paula Jean, did not bemoan her fate. Nor did she curse God or wonder "what might have been." This had been given to her and she would do her job joyfully. In those eighteen years, this young man, who could not move on his own, never developed a bed-sore. The story of Aaron and Paula Jean is a story of human endurance and receipt of the gift of grace. I ask you to contrast it to the vision of "peace" promulgated by the euthanasia doctor who extols how "beautiful" are the handicapped newborns who have been killed intentionally. These are two contrasting visions of our shared human future, one in which human beings will write the decisive chapter in whether we will abolish man — obliterate that which is truly human — or, by contrast, remember how to love and cherish our humanity, however wretched, however broken.

Attending to the Business That Is Ours

RICHARD JOHN NEUHAUS

I have always sensed that Robert Benne's work and mine are in close conversation and aimed at the same goal: A renewal of Christian confidence
in providing a morally informed philosophy for a more just and virtuous
society in the tradition of liberal democracy. I don't know if he would put it
that way. He can, and no doubt will continue to, speak for himself.

A book of this genre invites a looking back — a looking back that
helps us get our bearings for looking forward. I write in the aftermath of an
academic conference devoted to my book *The Naked Public Square*, which
was published in 1984. Any writer must be gratified when a book is
deemed worthy of such conversation more than two decades after its publication. Calvin is supposed to have said to a friend, "Today I have sent a
book off to the printer, there to perish like a beautiful rose dropped into a
very deep well, never to be heard from again." Such is the fate of most
books, although, it should be noted, not of Calvin's.

The Naked Public Square is an argument. Like most arguments, they
have to wait their time to get a hearing. My hunch is that books that become something of a point of reference appear at the edge of a time when a
lot of people have already intuitively arrived at the argument but haven't
quite put it together. Then comes along a book that elicits from readers
what the sociologist of knowledge Alfred Schutz called an Aha! experience. "But of course," they say. "That's just what I've been thinking."

To be sure, those who are unsympathetic to the argument are more
likely to say, "That's just what I suspected *they* were thinking." It is important to understand who was the "we" and who the "they" in the writing of

47

The Naked Public Square. In preparation for the above-mentioned conference at Princeton, I went back and reread the book in its entirety for the first time. It was as I thought, and as several participants in the conference pointed out. The authorial voice is typically pitched to the "we" of people familiar with the intellectual history and practice of liberal democracy. They were then and, for the most part, still are liberals of one kind or another. The emerging "they" of the time was what then was called and is still called "the religious right." The book was in large part a response to the question: What are "they" saying that "we" got wrong, and what should be done about it?

Decades later, many of those who were once "they" are now "we." It is a mark of the intellectual integrity and courage of people such as Robert Benne that they were not intimidated when the formerly taken-for-granted "we" accused them of having taken the side of the despised "they." It may be hard for some people to remember that not very long ago in the political class it was almost unanimously agreed that the ultimate insult was to call someone a conservative. Liberal revisionists who suggested that "those conservatives" might have a point or two went to great pains to make clear that they were not wandering from the liberal flock.

The growing public influence of politically engaged Christians who made no bones about being conservative has, since the 1980s, been accompanied by their immersion in the theory and practice of democratic politics. Theirs is no longer simply an aggressive defense against those who once made up the rules that excluded them. Twenty years ago, the very phrase "religion and public life" was highly controversial. In that combination, they were fighting words. In 1984 when I established the Center on Religion and Society, which would later become the Institute on Religion and Public Life and the publisher of *First Things,* there were in the country four or five such think tanks or academic programs. Today there are numerous institutes, academic centers, and publications dealing with religion and public life, including the fine program launched by Robert Benne at Roanoke College. They have been established on what is now the almost taken-for-granted premise that we cannot understand this society or sustain this polity without engaging the cultural and religious dynamics that shape the "We, the People" that is the locus of political sovereignty.

As many of the former "they" are now "we," so also many of the "we" are less worried about being viewed as "they." Those who are most militantly committed to the ideology of the naked public square have of late taken to raising alarums about the threat of "neoconservatives," "theoconservatives," and even of "theocrats." This is for the most part the last gasp — although it may be a very long last gasp — of those who would deny the self-evident truth that this constitutional order is not sustainable apart from the cultural, moral, and religious expression of the self-evident truths on which it is founded. Of course, I may be wrong. That denial may yet prevail. The Founders regularly called this order an experiment, and experiments can fail as well as succeed.

The reemergence of religion and religiously grounded moral argument in our public life will always entail the danger, just as critics charge, of people imposing their moral judgment on others. Democratic deliberation leads to decisions, and decisions backed by law are viewed as an imposition by those who disagree with those decisions. So it has always been. The charm of democracy is that most decisions are for the time being, and those who disagree will get their innings. Democracy is not only procedural — and it must be kept in mind that the procedural itself rests upon the foundation of commitment to certain moral goods — but it is very importantly procedural. The procedure is less about imposing than about proposing and persuading, and thus arriving at provisional resolutions in the form of a political equilibrium that is always for the time being.

How we propose and persuade raises the question of "public reason." In the minds of many, there is still a dichotomy, sometimes an antithesis, between public reason, on the one hand, and anything associated with religion on the other. I am persuaded that we live in a universally graced creation in which human reason participates in the mind of God and is capable of ascertaining moral truth and making moral arguments accessible to all reasonable persons.

This, too summarily stated, makes possible the kind of natural law reasoning so elegantly proposed today by John Finnis, Robert George, and other scholars. While what Finnis calls "ideal epistemic conditions" seldom obtain, most, if not all, of the questions pertinent to politics in a limited state ought to be resolvable by moral reason — whether or not called natural law — that is accessible to all. This assumption is behind the statement attributed to Luther, "I would rather be ruled by a wise Turk than a stupid Christian." (As it happens, I have conducted a search, and enlisted others in a search, for where Luther actually said that. Apparently he didn't, although the statement is consonant with his understanding of the twofold rule of God, sometimes called "two kingdoms.")

In the aberrations and contingencies of the world as it is, however, I am inclined to be skeptical about the possibility of agreeing on clear rules in determining what counts as public reason. Short of the final coming of the Kingdom of God, it is probable that we can at best arrive at a kind of modus vivendi that will not satisfy the intellectually fastidious. We could do worse than to settle for a vibrant democratic contestation in which moral reason and natural law arguments play an important part. Here I find myself in agreement with Eric Gregory of Princeton who said this at the aforementioned conference:

> Where are we to find the bases for "a defense of radical equality of men and women"? Finnis claims "nowhere better than the developed Christian teaching." I wonder, however, given the world in which we live, if we might better answer: Wherever we can find it! We do not need to agree on our theories of morality in order to sustain democratic practices and institutions. Does the moral health of democracy depend upon the adequacy of meta-ethical positions or reaching agreement on them? I hope not. Affirming this kind of political pluralism does not entail affirming pluralism in one's theory of value or embracing moral skepticism. We Christians, I would suggest, are not chiefly interested in protecting the philosophical bases of our ethical theories. Our concern is protecting the neighbor who comes our way.

I suppose some may think that smacks of intellectual despair, or even cynicism. Others, intending it as blame, may say that I am more of an Augustinian than a Thomist, and there is something to that. Ours is a fallen world in which reason is not just wounded but gravely wounded, albeit, thank God, not to the point of total corruption. By reason we entice from reason the best of which reason is capable, knowing that undisciplined passions will time and again deprive us of reason's full fruit. Meanwhile, in this robust democratic contestation we avail ourselves of available reasonable arguments, popular aspirations, rational fears, and motivating visions — so long as they are not dishonest or debasing — in order to achieve a closer approximation of justice, which is the virtue most proper to politics.

The word "meanwhile" is critically important. As the Letter to the Hebrews reminds us, we have here no abiding city but live toward the promised New Jerusalem. Christians and Jews who share that hope form a band of happy warriors without illusions. One is reminded of the words of St. Augustine: "Whenever you are as certain about something as I am, go forward with me; whenever you hesitate, seek with me; whenever you discover that you have gone wrong, come back to me; or, if I have gone wrong, call me back to you. In this way, we will travel along the street of love together as we make our way toward Him of whom it is said, 'Seek His face always.'"

This is the pact of truth and love that binds together those who seek his face always while seeking here on earth what justice may be possible. Not everybody seeks his face, and many, in both theory and practice, despair of justice. In the robust democratic contestation, we never forget that, in the words of St. Paul, we are also contending against the principalities and powers of the present disordered time.

In "East Coker" Eliot writes, "For us there is only the trying, the rest is not our business." These are not words of resignation but of gratitude. We are not God. Thank God we are not God. In the long run of history, when the experiment that is this constitutional order is succeeded by something better, or something worse, we will be asked whether we tried. When, please God, many years from now, people look back at the life and work of Robert Benne, I am confident that they will agree with the judgment that occasions this *Festschrift:* He tried, and our trying is greatly encouraged and enriched by his.

The Lutheran Necessity in Public Theology

The Lutheran Difference

JAMES NUECHTERLEIN

If you live long enough, and move around often enough, there are some things you get to know pretty well. A lifetime of Sundays in church as a member of some ten different congregations has given me extensive acquaintance with Lutheran theology and piety. It would mark me as particularly obtuse not to have by now a reasonably good sense of what it is that Lutherans are all about.

Yet I know about Lutherans not simply, or even primarily, because I have lived for seventy years among them, but because I am so thoroughly one of them. I became a Lutheran through accident of birth, but I remain one by conviction. The Lutheran take on the Christian faith — or at least a certain take on that take — informs my understanding of the world as does nothing else. It shapes my construction of reality, of how the world makes sense. It is from the inside out, as it were, that I can presume to say that I know Lutheranism. Perhaps on this occasion some exploration of my experiences living and worshipping as a Lutheran — experiences that, I trust, are not wholly idiosyncratic — may provide illumination that is more than merely personal.

I

My Christianity was formed in the Lutheran Church–Missouri Synod, and that has made all the difference. I do not, to be sure, affirm as an adult all the LCMS verities I uncritically accepted as a child — not a few of them I explicitly reject — but the piety in which I was raised remains indelibly with me. The LCMS not only provided the credal essentials, interpreted in the light of the Lutheran Confessions, that still define my theological universe, it imbued in me a cast of mind antecedent to, and deeper than, specific theological formulations.

One hears of "cultural Catholics," those who, whatever their attitude toward Catholic doctrine, retain a sense of Catholic identity. It strikes me that if there is such a thing as "cultural Lutheranism," it consists in an inclination toward unsentimental analysis of the human condition. To be a Missouri Synod Lutheran in my childhood was to be a serious person: to be, not cynical, but undeceived. We threw ourselves as radically as we did on God's grace because we knew as intensely as we did the reality of sin — sin not simply as susceptibility to the passions but as fundamental alienation from the will of God. It was, we knew, the disordered longings of our hearts that turned us inward on ourselves rather than outward to God and those around us.

The catechetical and worship experiences of my youth at Trinity Lutheran Church in Detroit focused on the ultimate consolation of the gospel message, but that consolation, we were clearly given to understand, dissolved into sentimentality without a steady sense of what it was that the gospel saved us *from*. No illusions for us about human nature, no nonsense about innate innocence gone wrong because of environment or social arrangements.

Sin was real and personal, and its consequence was death and separation from God, a death and separation overcome only in the crucifixion and resurrection of Jesus Christ. And our reconciliation with God, though accomplished in time, would be made perfect only in eternity. We were, by grace through faith and by virtue of our baptisms, new beings in Christ, but the final obliteration of the Old Adam would take place only in the End Time. In the meantime we were, though ultimately redeemed (we were not Manicheans), still marked by sin.

As sinners in a fallen world, believing that the infinitely better awaited us on the other side of death, we experienced life as the time in-between. Life of course held bountiful joys and graces, and not to love it would be a sign of ingratitude toward God. But we worried about its enticements — far more, I now think, than we needed to — and expected from it only imperfect fulfillment. Faith and family were what mattered and what one clung to for meaning and guidance; the world beyond was an uncertain and often chancy place. We were Christians of Augustinian persuasion, knowing that on earth we had no abiding city, that all our cities were greater or lesser Babylons through which we passed as strangers and pilgrims, alien residents on the journey to our citizenship in the New Jerusalem.

I do not mean to suggest that we were politically estranged from our country. Most members of the LCMS were in fact deeply patriotic. But neither politics nor patriotism was of ultimate concern. Politics might involve us deeply, but we were securely inoculated against its utopian and salvific temptations. It could provide at its best for a very rough justice, and while that was not nothing, neither was it worthy of total commitment.

It seems to me in retrospect that the somewhat un-American nature of the Lutheranism of my childhood made its adherents accordingly safe for patriotism. We could love America — feel toward it that gratitude, pride, and affection that is natural for people to extend to their homeland — without being tempted to the idolatrous nationalism that has deformed so much of modern history. How could we make an idol of a nation whose philosophical assumptions (enlightenment liberalism), dominant religious tradition (evangelical Calvinism), and prevailing spirit (romantic optimism) were in so many ways alien to our most basic understandings? Because we were in a deep sense strangers in America, we could be safely at home there.

What eased our otherness was our standing, however uncertain, as Protestants. (We were uneasy Protestants because we tended to view most other heirs of the Reformation as susceptible to various strains of pietistic enthusiasm and doctrinal undependability.) Mainstream Protestantism still constituted the vital center of American religious culture in the 1940s and '50s. Although Lutherans were located some distance from the center of that center — which was occupied, more or less in order, by Episcopalians, Presbyterians, Methodists, and Congregationalists — we were still part of the grand anti-papist communion. Catholic otherness was so much more Other than our own.

It is difficult to recall today how much of Lutheran identity in those years consisted in anti-Catholicism. It pervaded my childhood: Reformation Day celebrations (exceeded in importance only by Easter and Christmas) that were unabashed exercises in Protestant triumphalism, the "Why I Am Not a Catholic" tracts in the church narthex, Saturday afternoons in Fall rooting for Southern Methodist to crush Notre Dame in football, and, as I got into my teens, the inevitable first question from my mother about any new date, "She's not Catholic, is she?"

It would be too easy to dismiss that anti-Catholicism simply as un-thinking prejudice. It was rather, as were so many of Missouri's flaws, an offshoot of its intense preoccupation with doctrine. The German immi-grants who founded the LCMS in the 1840s were appalled by what seemed to them the theological slovenliness that marked American Christianity (including much of American Lutheranism). They developed, in reaction, an extraordinary emphasis on right belief that persisted intact a century later. The central doctrine to be preserved from corruption, of course, was the touchstone of the Reformation: justification by grace alone through faith alone because of Christ alone. Everything depended on that, and Catholics, according to everything we were taught — this was, remember, pre–Vatican II — didn't have it right.

In fact — and this was the real, if mostly unacknowledged, center of the piety I absorbed — nobody outside of Missouri had it entirely right. We weren't just anti-Catholic; we were opposed to pretty much everything beyond our carefully patrolled confessional borders. In our circles, refer-ences to the Church and to the Missouri Synod were largely interchange-able. Official doctrine spoke of a trans-denominational invisible Church, of which only God had full knowledge. But most of us were tacitly per-suaded that, at its manifestation following Christ's return in glory, the in-visible Church would turn out to be populated in very large part by Mis-souri Synod Lutherans. Who else, after all, had sufficient hold on the doctrinal precision surely required for admission to the Kingdom? We were in practice the sectarians that our Lutheran Confessions insisted we were not.

II

My post-childhood theological development has essentially been an exer-cise in complexifying, though not entirely repudiating, what I learned in my Missouri Synod youth. The net effect of my religious experience over the decades — including membership in a variety of congregations di-vided almost equally between the LCMS and the Evangelical Lutheran Church in America (or one of its predecessors) — has been to leave me more thoroughly Lutheran than ever, though sometimes in ways quite dis-tant from my childhood piety.

I am, to begin with, far more catholic (even if only lower case) than I could once have imagined. It was as a student at Valparaiso University (an independent Lutheran university with historic ties to the LCMS) that I first encountered the idea that Lutherans might have more in common with Catholics than with most Protestants. The idea struck me, at first, as theologically absurd, but over time it came to make a great deal of sense.

The most obvious point of affinity with Catholics, of course, was our mutual emphasis on sacramental theology. It took a lot of de-Protestantizing for me to come to a full appreciation of the Eucharist. It was not that we took holy communion lightly in my childhood. Quite the contrary. Our reverence for it was so great that we worried about debasing it by overuse. My congregation, typical in its practice, offered communion once a month. My family, again typically, participated every other month. To commune monthly was to appear over-zealous in piety, or, even more, to invite suspicion concerning some terrible guilt in one's life.

My experience at Valparaiso and then in parishes shepherded by clergy educated in the liturgical renewal movement taught me to understand the Eucharist as the proper focus of worship. On the two occasions early in our marriage when my wife and I were members of congregations that did not offer weekly communion, we agitated for change. I believe as a general principle that congregations should not have major liturgical change thrust upon them, but regular availability of the Eucharist became for me an issue that could not be compromised. Even as a child it had occurred to me that concern about overuse of communion could with equal logic apply to repeated recitation of the Lord's Prayer and the Apostles' or Nicene creeds — indeed to structured worship of any sort.

Affinity for traditional liturgical practices — for the ancient patterns of worship still common among Anglicans, Catholics, and the Eastern Orthodox — marked me from young adulthood on as a Lutheran of evangelical catholic persuasion. An orthodox liturgy, I came to understand, is a bulwark against heresy; in it, the deposit of faith from across the centuries maintains its living witness. High churchmanship has its own temptations — fussiness, snobbery, aestheticism — but maintaining continuity of worship with those who have preceded us in the faith more than justifies the risks.

My de-Protestantizing never went so far as to eliminate my childhood preoccupation with the sermon. My father was a careful student and critic of the art of preaching, and it was a rare Sunday on which the first topic of family conversation after church was not an evaluation of how well or badly the pastor had performed. I have, unfortunately, inherited my father's critical homiletical instinct, and my wife occasionally has to remind me that it is not the best approach to worship to act as if one were on assignment from the drama desk at the *New York Times*.

The sermons of my Missouri Synod youth had, if nothing else, the virtue of predictability. The three-point formula was securely in place. The pastor reminded us, every Sunday, that we were sinners deserving of eternal punishment and separation from God, that Christ had died to save us from the consequences of our sins, and that we should in gratitude lead lives that reflected his sacrificial love for us.

Point two in this catechetical exercise received the fullest elaboration. I grew up assuming that all properly constructed sermons included a full exposition of our inability to make compensation for our sins and of Christ's substitutionary atonement for that sin on the Cross. The emphasis throughout was on a rigorously precise understanding of the gospel as grace alone appropriated through faith alone — which, we were given to understand, is what distinguished Lutheran doctrinal purity from sin-obsessed fundamentalism on the one hand and works-beguiled Romanism on the other. The sermon was intended less to apply the gospel to our lives than to instruct us in its proper meaning: not how shall we then live but how should we rightly believe.

One seldom encounters the three-point sermon anymore, and that, for the most part, is cause for gratitude. Familiarity breeds inattention, and there are better things for pastors to do with sermon time than go over yet again what even the dullest parishioner mastered in confirmation instruction. Good preaching does many things, but catechesis is not chief among them.

Still, as I discovered in congregational settings far removed from Missouri Synod certainties, preachers can do worse than rely on formulas. Better a pat orthodoxy than inventive heresy. One of my pastors — thoughtful, intelligent, personable — had just one significant drawback. He was, judging at least from his sermons, without faith in the gospel. He preached not grace but an accusing moralism: he specialized in well-crafted sermons denouncing comfortable piety and placid conformity. One Sunday he announced that only those thoroughly determined to transform their lives should avail themselves of the Eucharist. A temptation common among Lutheran pastors is to preach Hallmark theology — gospel without law. He was the only one I've ever encountered who consistently did the reverse. I was relieved for both of us when he left the pastorate to go into counseling.

It is a blessing to report that in a lifetime of church attendance I have heard far more good preaching than bad. Beyond that, my only confident generalization about sermons is that they are shorter than they used to be: few Lutheran pastors today preach more than twenty minutes, a considerable reduction from the twenty-five to thirty-five minutes that was common in my youth.

The good preaching I have heard follows no clear pattern: effective sermons come in styles long and short, polished and plain, analytical and narrative. Theological sophistication helps, but is not in itself determinative. Few young pastors, even those with excellent seminary training, preach really well. Only extended experience of life — especially experience that involves suffering — produces the intelligence of the heart that great preachers possess. I take it as no accident that two of the most effective preachers I have known were recovering alcoholics.

Preaching improves with humility. I have on more than one occasion felt the effect of an otherwise admirable sermon ruined by the sense that the pastor had been told once too often what a fine preacher he was. One wants a pastor whom life has taught to preach grace, who knows what it means to pray, "Lord, be merciful to me, a sinner." I recall from many years ago the farewell sermon of a Missouri Synod preacher of the old school. His had been a modest pastoral career, but he wanted us to know that he left the pulpit with no regrets. "I have always," he said, "preached Christ and him crucified." That was all, and that was enough.

My continuing theological education in homiletics, the sacraments, and related matters took place in a variety of congregational settings, some within the LCMS, some not. My initial venture beyond the confines of Missouri was a matter of necessity: my first college teaching assignment took me to a town where the local LCA (Lutheran Church in America) parish was the only Lutheran congregation within fifty miles. In later years, dispiriting institutional developments within the Lutheran church turned me into a "congregational Lutheran." I developed the practice, whenever I changed location, of joining the local parish in which I felt most at home, without regard to its church-wide affiliation.

I would not presume, on the basis of my happenstance congregational experience, to offer comparative judgments on the LCMS and the ELCA. (I can note for what it's worth that my two favorite congregations over a lifetime were a tiny ELCA parish in New York City and my present very large LCMS congregation in Valparaiso, Indiana.) The relevant point for me was that, in institutional terms, neither the ELCA or the LCMS offered a particularly congenial home for the kind of Lutheran I had become.

My status on the Lutheran margins became clarified during the several years, beginning in the mid-1990s, in which I was privileged to serve on the board of the American Lutheran Publicity Bureau. The ALPB was created in 1914 to help German Lutheran immigrants adjust to life in America and, more broadly, to establish connections between Lutheranism and the larger American culture. It continues today as an independent, pan-Lutheran renewal organization of evangelical catholic inclination. Its members and supporters think of Lutheranism as a confessional movement within the one Church of Christ. They are at once ecumenical in spirit — they cannot, for example, imagine any sane definition of the Christian reality that excludes Catholicism — and committed to the distinctive Lutheran construal of the Christian faith.

In my years with the ALPB I worked closely with pastors of both the LCMS and the ELCA, and I discovered among both groups a significant degree of estrangement from their church bodies. Those in the LCMS worried about what they saw as the synod's continuing sectarian inclinations and its tendency to biblicist obscurantism. The LCMS tore itself apart in the early 1970s in a bitter struggle over the interpretation of Scripture. LCMS conservatives, who won the struggle, insist on a belief in verbal inspiration that makes the Bible incapable of error on any point and requires that it be read as expressing literal truth on all matters to which it addresses itself, whether or not those matters are of intrinsic theological significance. The moderates who lost out understand the doctrines of biblical infallibility and inerrancy to refer to issues essential to orthodox belief, and they resist the notion that skepticism over, say, the historicity of Adam and Eve undermines scriptural authority. They worry that Missouri will sacrifice its long tradition of serious confessional orthodoxy to its neo-fundamentalist temptations.

The ELCA pastors had a quite different set of concerns. They feared that their church body — created in 1987 in a merger of the LCA, the ALC (American Lutheran Church), and a small group of breakaway Missouri moderates — was drifting from its Lutheran theological moorings and merging into the liberal Protestant mainstream. They complained of church and seminary leadership in thrall to prevailing liberationist, feminist, and multiculturalist fashions and of race-and-gender quota systems that owe more to contemporary elite social opinion than to the Lutheran tradition. They saw, in sum, a church body reenacting, in alarmingly rapid fashion, the unhappy history of liberal American Protestantism.

My experience in the ALPB confirmed my sense of the current Lutheran condition. There remain, at the congregational level, large numbers of parishes in which orthodox faith, sacramental integrity, sound preaching, and the impulses of charity live and flourish. But both major church bodies display at their center signs of decay and fatigue that invite, if not quite despair, a widespread melancholy.

The melancholy goes deep. The most fundamental division in evangelical catholic circles is between those who are determined, come what may, to remain Lutheran and those who are at least willing to consider that their catholicity might one day edge into Catholicism. The issue, at heart, is how one defines the church.

The evangelical catholic Lutherans I know who have gone to Rome — and I know a distressingly large number of them — have done so, if I understand them rightly, for mostly ecclesiastical reasons. They think Rome has clear claim, in the West at least, to the title of the one, holy, catholic, and apostolic Church. Evangelical catholics of my persuasion think of the Church in different terms. We consider that the one Church has had various institutional manifestations through time, and we find our distinct Lutheran piety fully compatible with the Great Tradition of Christian orthodoxy that is embodied within, but finally transcends, particular ecclesial arrangements.

I have, I confess, lingering negative reasons for declining Rome's invitation. Many of the sixteenth-century quarrels between the reformers and the Holy See have been resolved in recent years — most notably in the Joint Declaration on the Doctrine of Justification (1999) — but on certain critical issues, such as the relation between justification and sanctification or between Scripture and tradition, differences remain that, however subtle, are not insignificant.

There are, moreover, a number of post-Reformation issues that separate most evangelical catholics from Rome: papal infallibility, the Marian dogmas, ordination of women, contraception. Traditionalist Catholics rightly complain of a cafeteria approach to church doctrine in which presumably loyal members of the church practice personal discretion in deciding which teachings they will or will not accept as binding on them. It would be a dishonorable act and a grave violation of conscience to seek communion in the Roman Catholic Church while harboring a host of mental reservations as to the Church's dogma. As I regularly explain to those who ask about my own situation, better a good Lutheran than a bad Catholic.

And the fact that I am a good Lutheran is finally what matters.

III

Lutherans hold no monopoly on the doctrine of justification by which, we have always insisted, the Church stands or falls. What remains distinctively Lutheran is the setting of that doctrine in a dialectical theological framework. The Lutheran dialectic takes a variety of forms: the emphasis on the law/gospel distinction as interpretive principle and theological guide; the understanding of social ethics and responsibilities according to the doctrine of the Two Kingdoms; the conception of the human condition as essentially *simul* — we are at once, Luther insisted, sinners and saints, enemies of God and yet fully redeemed participants in his eternal glory.

I affirm these distinctively Lutheran perspectives because I believe they conform to the reality of our lives. They fit the rough contrariness of our experience; they are at once contradictory and true. We yearn to be followers of God even as we rebel against his injunctions. The Lutheran *simul* captures our reality better than do visions of perfection or divinization or anticipation of the eschaton. Lutheranism engages us in our doubled condition and reminds us of its founder's central insight, confessed as he died, that we are all beggars before God. Day by day, Luther declared, we die and rise again. There is no straight line toward the beatific vision. There is only the perennial reminder of our baptismal identity: He who gave us life will, in the face of all our perversities, call us back to himself.

These understandings are not exclusive to Lutheranism. They are part of the Christian patrimony. St. Paul wrote in his letter to the Romans of the good that he would that he did not and of the evil that he would not that he did. But it is within the Lutheran tradition that the antinomies of the faith have been kept most vibrantly alive.

I remain a Lutheran because I find its understanding of the human reality and the divine dispensation persuasive. I am tempted to despair because the Lutheran sensibility seems variously at risk in its current institutional manifestations and I find it difficult to imagine how things might be turned around. But that, I remind (and console) myself, is not my business. Only gratitude is.

The Lutheran Corrective

GILBERT MEILAENDER

When Robert Benne composed his "theological autobiography" for the journal *Dialog* in 2003, he used the occasion to recall his encounters over the years with many great theologians — many of them Lutherans — of the twentieth century.[1] Near the end of his reminiscences Benne notes an irony: During the course of all these years he had never met or heard either Reinhold or Richard Niebuhr; yet their influence on him had been more substantial than the many great thinkers whom he had met.

Perhaps it will not be amiss, therefore, if I begin with yet another great thinker whom, simply because their lives did not overlap, Benne could not have met. In one of his journal entries, Søren Kierkegaard writes:

> Lutheranism is a corrective — but a corrective made into the norm, the whole, is *eo ipso* confusing in the next generation (when that which it was meant to correct no longer exists). And as long as this continues things get worse with every generation, until in the end the corrective produces the exact opposite of what was originally intended.
>
> And such, moreover, is the case. Taken by itself, as the whole of Christianity, the Lutheran corrective produces the most subtle type of worldliness and paganism.[2]

1. Robert Benne, "Brushes with the Great and Near-Great: Fifty Years of Theological Reminiscences," *Dialog* 42 (Spring, 2003): 86-90.
2. *The Journals of Søren Kierkegaard*, ed. and trans. Alexander Dru (London and Glasgow: Collins Fontana Books, 1958), pp. 232-33.

66

Looking around, after a lifetime devoted to the Lutheran church's theological work, its social reflection, and its educational institutions, Benne might sometimes wonder whether Kierkegaard's judgment was not apt — distressing as such a thought might be when taking stock of one's important commitments.

Nevertheless, this is where Lutherans in America — on both the "left" and the "right" — find themselves today, and it is essential that we realize this if we are to find a helpful way into the future. Turning a "corrective" into a "norm," we have too often sought to construct an entire theology on the basis of some supposed distinctively Lutheran insight — most generally, some version of the distinction between law and gospel, sin and grace. And, alas, attempting to be distinctive can produce just the opposite. When no more can be said about the shape and form of the Christian life than that it is lived out in the tension between God's verdicts of condemnation and of forgiveness, we fall all too easily into that subtle worldliness and paganism Kierkegaard detected — unwilling to find direction for the Christian life in the will of God, yet moralistically (and all too stridently) taking our behavioral cues from the world around us. Or, alternatively, we piously fear to say much about the shape a life empowered by the gospel ought to take, lest we should somehow not let forgiveness have the last word. In either case, we do not "strive," as the author of Hebrews puts it (12:14), "for the holiness without which no one will see the Lord."

If this is where Lutherans in America for the most part find themselves today, we cannot lay the blame at Robert Benne's doorstep. Although he has worked diligently to unfold a distinctively Lutheran understanding of the Christian life — and even though I myself would say that our most pressing task for the moment is not to focus on such distinctiveness — he has been clear that what he is sketching is, in Kierkegaard's terms, a correction, not a norm. Lutheranism for him has been a particular way of reading and interpreting the world of Christian convictions — a world Lutherans received and did not create. Hence, for him and quite explicitly, "Lutheran perspectives operating without the larger context of the great tradition are finally anemic."[3]

One way to see the importance of this is to look at institutions; for they can retain a specifically Christian character only if they find ways to

---

3. Robert Benne, *Ordinary Saints: An Introduction to the Christian Life*, 2nd ed. (Minneapolis: Fortress Press, 2003), p. 18.

embody both theological vision and moral ethos into their structure. If they display a Lutheran "allergy to law," they will be unable to shape their common life in ways that accord with Christian tradition. It is not accidental, I suspect, that in recent years Benne turned his attention to the difficulties church-related colleges and universities have had in retaining their heritage.[4]

Quite often I have tried on others the following thought experiment: Suppose one were to spend a week immersed in the life of each of the following four institutions: University of Notre Dame, Wheaton College, Calvin College, and Valparaiso University.[5] I suspect that after just a week one would be able to say something fairly specific about the character (shaped by their respective Christian traditions) of Notre Dame, of Wheaton, and of Calvin. (To be sure, one might like or not like that character, be drawn to it or repelled by it. That does not matter for purposes of the thought experiment. What matters is that there would be a shape, a form, to the life of the place.) I also suspect that one would have a much harder time depicting anything religiously distinctive about Valparaiso. Lutheran theology — and Lutheran scholars and administrators — have seemed unable or unwilling to fashion an institution shaped by their theological perspective.[6]

Might it be that this form of "anemia" results from turning a correction into a norm? On Benne's account, the problem these colleges face in retaining identity is primarily the problem of resisting secularization. But what if Lutheran theology — in those modes in which it understands itself as norm rather than correction, as free-standing rather than as one way of understanding the great Christian tradition — invites such secularization? Thus, Mark Edwards, at a time when he was president of St. Olaf College, could write: "Church-related higher education is called to employ reason to pursue truth with all the intellectual rigor at its command. There should be in most cases no substantive difference between scholarship by Chris-

---

4. Robert Benne, *Quality with Soul: How Six Premier Colleges and Universities Keep Faith with Their Religious Traditions* (Grand Rapids: Eerdmans, 2001).

5. These are, in fact, four of the six institutions Benne profiles in *Quality with Soul*. The other two are Baylor University and St. Olaf College.

6. Here I depart somewhat from Benne's own characteristically generous judgment. He says of all six institutions profiled that "the Christian account of life and reality [is] made visible and relevant in all facets of each school's activities — academic, extra-curricular, music and the arts, worship, atmosphere, and self-definition. In other words, the schools have both quality and soul, bound up together." Benne, *Quality with Soul*, p. 95.

tians and by non-Christians."[7] It is not hard to understand how with such a view — interpreting Lutheranism as committed to the position that Christian faith makes no intellectual difference — we might well have difficulty shaping an institution with a specifically Christian character. The effects of the faith, if any, will be solely interior. Lutherans have come to grant that such an understanding of their tradition did not serve them well politically in the twentieth century. Nor will it serve their educational institutions well.

Interestingly, on Benne's account, Valparaiso did not begin with such a narrow understanding of its Lutheran character. O. P. Kretzmann's guiding vision in the university's most formative years "was informed by a Christian humanism more akin to the Catholic approach than to dialectical Lutheranism. Confident in the Christian account of life and reality . . . the university aimed at a synthesis of Christ and culture."[8] In more recent years, however, the predominant language at the university has been that of "Athens and Jerusalem." That coordinating conjunction "and" simply places two realities side-by-side, without seeking any synthesis. If this does not immediately lead to Kierkegaard's "paganism," it can scarcely fail to lead to the "worldliness" he also remarked upon.

All that said, the central focus of Robert Benne's work has not been analysis of colleges; it has been the moral life, the discipline of Christian ethics, and the need for Christian faith to shape culture. And here too we can and should say that "Lutheran perspectives operating without the larger context of the great tradition are finally anemic." I want to illustrate this by focusing briefly on one very important moral conflict that has been a matter of deep dispute within the church, within civil society, and within our political institutions during much of Robert Benne's career as a Christian ethicist: namely, the matter of abortion.

This is a helpful place to focus our attention, for it would be strange, I think, to suppose that there should be a peculiarly Lutheran position on abortion. Just as when the Lutheran Reformers, in the twenty-eight articles of the Augsburg Confession, outlined their basic stance on matters of *faith*, the first three topics they addressed were simply central themes of the catholic tradition which they shared (the Triune God; original sin; Jesus as

---

7. Mark U. Edwards Jr., "Christian Colleges: A Dying Light or a New Refraction?" *Christian Century* 116 (April 21-28, 1999): 461.

8. Benne, *Quality with Soul,* p. 135.

the Son of God), so also there are *moral* perspectives and insights every bit as early and as deeply embedded in the Christian tradition.

Consider the shared Christian teaching and vision that Lutherans inherited, and which they did not seek to correct. One of the things that strikingly separated the first Christians from much of their surrounding culture was their condemnation of abortion and infanticide. So, for example, in the famous depiction of Christian life as a choice between two ways, the way of life and the way of death, which appears in a second-century document usually called the Didache, we find the injunction: "do not murder a child by abortion or kill a newborn infant."[9] In his *History of European Morals from Augustus to Charlemagne*, W. E. H. Lecky noted that, with respect to abortion, "the language of the Christians from the very beginning was widely different" from that of the culture in which they found themselves. "With unwavering consistency and with the strongest emphasis, they denounced the practice, not simply as inhuman, but as definitely murder. In the penitential discipline of the Church, abortion was placed in the same category as infanticide. . . ."[10]

That moral judgment was dependent, as David Jones has recently developed in detail, upon the view — almost universally held for at least the first three centuries by Christians in both the Greek-speaking East and the Latin-speaking West — that the child in the womb is one of us from the time of conception.[11] In later centuries that understanding was made more complicated in the Latin-speaking West by the influence of Aristotelian biology and its distinction between formed and unformed embryos (a distinction that never gained a foothold among Christians in the East).

Since the sixteenth century, Protestant Reformers were quite willing to rethink and to "correct" aspects of the church's tradition that seemed to have gone awry, especially if those aspects had not been prominent in the first centuries of the church's existence. Neither Luther nor Calvin retained that medieval distinction between formed and unformed embryos. Luther tended toward what is called "traducianism" — the view that the soul, to-

9. *Early Christian Fathers*, trans. and ed. Cyril C. Richardson, The Library of Christian Classics, vol. 1 (Philadelphia: Westminster Press, 1953), p. 172.

10. W. E. H. Lecky, *History of European Morals from Augustus to Charlemagne*, vol. 2 (London: Longmans, Green, and Co., 1911), p. 22.

11. David Albert Jones, *The Soul of the Embryo: An Enquiry into the Status of the Human Embryo in the Christian Tradition* (London and New York: Continuum, 2004).

gether with the body, is generated and handed on to the child by the parents who conceive it. Calvin was drawn more to the view that the soul is newly created by God for each human being, but as Jones puts it, Calvin "saw no reason to follow the Aristotelian view that the soul was infused at 40 days or thereabouts. He held rather that the soul was created and infused at the moment of conception."[12]

This high view of the status of the embryo, so firmly grounded in the first centuries of the church's life, was not, however, the product of embryological investigation alone. It was influenced by the simple fact that Christians worshiped one who had been born as a baby to a mother Mary, whom they called the "Mother of God." Even while her son was in the womb, Mary had been greeted by her relative Elizabeth, in the well-known story recounted in Luke chapter one, with the words: "Why is this granted me, that the mother of my Lord should come to me?"

That story of Mary and Elizabeth, of a baby in a manger, has penetrated the center of Christian consciousness. As G. K. Chesterton put it, Christian literature and art — both elite and popular — have "rung the changes on that single paradox; that the hands that had made the sun and stars were too small to reach the huge heads of the cattle." It would be difficult to overestimate the influence of that image. As Chesterton again put it: "Every Catholic child has learned from pictures, and even every Protestant child from stories, this incredible combination of contrasted ideas as one of the very first impressions on his mind."[13] Every child who has ever known "a real Christmas" will have "whether he likes it or not, an association in his mind between two ideas that most of mankind must regard as remote from each other; the idea of a baby and the idea of unknown strength that sustains the stars."[14]

This sense of the wonder of the Christmas story — that Mary should have carried in her womb the one whose word brought into existence and sustains all that is — was, therefore, deeply embedded in the Christian tradition that shaped the piety of Martin Luther. Thus, for example, one stanza of a brief carol he wrote for his children at Christmas goes in English translation:

12. Jones, *The Soul of the Embryo*, p. 146.
13. G. K. Chesterton, *The Everlasting Man* (Garden City, NY: Image Books, 1955), p. 168.
14. Chesterton, *Everlasting Man*, p. 169.

What the globe could not enwrap
Nestled lies in Mary's lap.
Just a baby, very wee,
Yet Lord of all the world is he.[15]

"Luther is at his best and most characteristic," Roland Bainton writes, "in his sermons on the Nativity."[16] An example: "Let us, then, meditate upon the Nativity just as we se it happening in our own babies. Behold Christ lying in the lap of his young mother. . . . Look at the Child, knowing nothing. Yet all that is belongs to him. . . . To me there is no greater consolation given to mankind than this, that Christ became man, a child, a babe, playing in the lap and at the breasts of his most gracious mother."[17]

Clearly, Protestants received — and sought simply to be faithful to and develop more fully — a Christian teaching that, locating the beginnings of every human life at conception, made abortion unthinkable. To be sure, Protestants brought to this discussion their own distinctive emphases, but these were used not to weaken or make anemic the vision of unborn children they had received, but, rather, to reinforce the catholic tradition.

Among the characteristic Protestant emphases was a particular understanding of the teaching that men and women had been created in "the image of God."[18] Over-simplifying just a bit, we can say that Christians have held two sorts of views about the meaning of this concept. One view, which might be called a "substantive" view, locates the *imago* in some attribute or feature of human nature: our rational capacities, for example, which permit human beings to exercise what Genesis calls "dominion" in the creation. The other view, which may be termed "relational," has understood the image as pointing to the fact that human beings are created to live in relation to God — addressed by God and called to respond to his address. Variants of this second kind of view have been an especially common emphasis among Protestants.

Luther and Calvin both tended to focus on the fact that human beings were created to live in "right relation" with God — in a perfect harmony in which their response to God's call was spontaneous and wholehearted.

15. Quoted in Roland H. Bainton, *Here I Stand: A Life of Martin Luther* (New York: Mentor Books, 1955), p. 237.
16. Bainton, *Here I Stand*, p. 276.
17. Quoted in Bainton, *Here I Stand*, p. 277.
18. See Jones, *The Soul of the Embryo*, pp. 149-51.

Karl Barth, the greatest Protestant theologian of the twentieth century, developed a relational understanding of the *imago*, depicting men and women as called to live in relation with God and with each other, even as the Triune God himself is from eternity a relation of Father, Son, and Spirit. Helmut Thielicke, a well-known twentieth-century Lutheran theologian, likewise argued that the *imago* referred primarily to a "state of relation" rather than to a "state of being."

This relational understanding has given Protestants a way to articulate an important Protestant theme: the priority of God's grace to our achievements. "The divine likeness," Thielicke writes, "rests on the fact that God remembers man."[19] The relation of the creature to the Creator, distorted and corrupted by sin, must be continually received anew as it is *given* in Christ. From this characteristically Protestant angle, therefore, the focus is on the grace by which God bestows and confers worth on us rather than on any intrinsic qualities or achievements that are ours. And once that becomes the lens through which we think about human status and standing, we will have reason not to depart from the received Christian evaluation of the unborn as equal in worth and dignity to the rest of us, but, on the contrary, to reinforce it.

This becomes even more evident when we focus on a second, related, characteristically Protestant emphasis. At the heart of much of the controversy with Roman Catholicism in the sixteenth century was an emphasis — first of all, Luther's — on our inability to please God through any effort or achievement of our own. In the technical language of Scripture and the dogmatic controversies of the time, Protestants insisted that human beings can be justified before God only by grace, through faith, for Christ's sake. Put more simply, we have no claims upon God, but must rely on his mercy and grace, which are entirely unmerited by us. Our dignity is not achieved but bestowed and conferred upon us by God. Hence, those of us whose capacities are great and whose achievements are many — those whom we celebrate with *Festschriften* and those able so to celebrate them! — have no more standing before God than those of us whose capacities and achievements are few.

The embryo and the fetus may have achieved little — though, in passing, we might marvel at how astonishing is their power of self-directed de-

19. Helmut Thielicke, *Theological Ethics*, volume I: *Foundations* (Philadelphia: Fortress Press, 1966), p. 165.

velopment — but that does not make their lives of any less worth before God. "What is this but to say," as Paul Ramsey once wrote, "that we are all fellow fetuses?"[20] All of us without the ability to speak for ourselves in the court that really counts — before God. All of us in need of a Vindicator to speak on our behalf.

This powerful Lutheran and, more generally, Protestant insight into the way in which all our claims to eminence and accomplishment, all our protestations of significance, all our confidence in our own virtue, cannot finally make any of us right or give any of us rights before God provides — from a somewhat different angle — powerful support for the shared Christian sense that the weak and vulnerable embryo, seemingly of little worth, is one of us. Its weakness and lack of distinction can scarcely be disqualifying when, in the one forum that really counts, we are no stronger or more distinguished.

In the end, perhaps we do well to return to that great Danish Lutheran thinker whom Robert Benne could not have met. He ended his life opposing a church that, treating a correction as if it were a norm, had, at least in his view, lost the culture-shaping power of Christian faith. And a part of that power, as Kierkegaard saw it, was that the mystery of Christian love depends not on any quality in the one who is loved but on the steadfast commitment of the one who loves.

> Suppose there were two artists. The one said, "I have travelled much and seen much in the world, but I have sought in vain to find a man worth painting. I have found no face with such perfection of beauty that I could make up my mind to paint it. In every face I have seen one or another little fault. Therefore I seek in vain." Would this indicate that this artist was a great artist? On the other hand, the second said, "Well, I do not pretend to be a real artist; neither have I travelled in foreign lands. But remaining in the little circle of men who are closest to me, I have not found a face so insignificant or so full of faults that I still could not discern in it a more beautiful side and discover something glorious. Therefore I am happy in the art I practise. It satisfied me without my making any claim to being an

20. Paul Ramsey, "Reference Points in Deciding about Abortion," in *The Morality of Abortion: Legal and Historical Perspectives,* ed. John T. Noonan Jr. (Cambridge, MA: Harvard University Press, 1970), p. 67.

artist." Would this not indicate that precisely this one was the artist, one who by bringing a certain something with him found then and there what the much-travelled artist did not find anywhere in the world, perhaps because he did not bring a certain something with him! Consequently the second of the two was the artist.[21]

It is for a church that could share such a vision, and for institutions shaped by that sort of church, that Robert Benne has written. We should ask first not whether this vision is distinctive, but whether it is true — and, then, whether we have the will to receive and act upon its truth.

21. Søren Kierkegaard, *Works of Love*, trans. Howard and Edna Hong (New York: Harper Torchbooks, 1962), pp. 156-57.

What Lutherans Have to Offer

Mark A. Noll

This tribute to Robert Benne tries to answer three questions that have been central to some of his most enduring concerns: Why would American Christians, and especially conservative Protestants, benefit in their political thought and activity from Lutheran insights? How could the theology of Martin Luther provide what American Christians need? Why, if Lutheran theology provides what American believers require, has there been such a meager Lutheran contribution to American political life?

*   *   *

Political activity by American Christian believers, especially Protestant evangelicals, has often been lacking exactly in those areas where Lutheran theology is strong. Despite considerable integrity at some times and places, the political activity of conservative Protestant evangelicals has been marked by several consistent weaknesses.

First is a preference for revivalistic political moralism over patient political discernment; evangelicals have been notable for mounting crusades, often around one issue (slavery or anti-slavery, temperance, anti-communism, anti-abortion), but have done less well at thinking about Christian political responsibility from the bottom up and acting with consistent Christian integrity over the political landscape as a whole.

Second, evangelicals have displayed a persistent eagerness to cry wolf at the expense of discriminating between the wolf in sheep's clothing and the sheep in wolf's clothing. The prime instance of this difficulty was probably the election of 1800 when conservative Protestants rallied against the election of Thomas Jefferson as if his victory would have cataclysmic effects of apocalyptic proportions. Similar panic swept the evangelical world in 1960 at the prospect of electing a Roman Catholic, John F. Kennedy, and in 1996 at the prospect of re-electing Bill Clinton. In none of these cases did anything like the worse fears of the fearful eventuate. On the other hand, evangelicals have also supported a number of leaders who professed something like evangelical faith, but who have performed in office with anything but a consistently Christian political ethic.

Third, evangelicals have often displayed a reluctance to admit that morally effective government cannot always be small government. Early in American history, a strong bond was cemented between Protestant churches and the republican principles of the new United States. Those principles emphasized the need for powerful checks to control the reach of central government. In the centuries since, conservative Protestants have retained those republican fears, but inconsistently. In particular, during recent decades they have been eager to cry "Big Government" when proposals are advanced that they do not like (like civil rights or universal health care), but reluctant to say anything when centralized government authority is brought to bear for causes they favor (like defending definitions of traditional marriage or prohibiting abortion on demand). The problem is not necessarily with the causes championed or opposed, but with the confusion introduced by claiming to be against Big Government in principle.

Fourth, evangelicals often have shown a predilection for confusing the history of the United States with the history of salvation. The long line of books, sermons, and speeches claiming to see a special providential destiny for the United States — beyond the care that divine providence has promised for all nations in all circumstances — has consistently put American Christians at risk of spiritual idolatry and national hubris.

Finally, American Christian believers of all sorts have been prone to confuse ultimate spiritual realities with secondary political ends. Times past counting in American history, energized believers have entered the public arena to advocate pet projects as if their success or failure meant the end of the world. In Christian terms, it is certain they have been wrong every time.

*   *   *

It is, of course, important to say that Christian political action in America, both past and present, does contain many bright spots, for there has been a great deal of good done in, to, and with the political process from professing Christian believers, and of many varieties. Yet the problems are serious.

As a way of moving toward a more responsible Christian politics, the theology of Martin Luther would seem to offer a better way. I say "seems" because it is not clear to me that Lutheran practice has ever fulfilled the promise of Luther's theology. But remaining for the moment with theology, we have with Luther a set of emphases that can provide healthy *motives* for being active politically (that is, guidance for why and how believers should be involved in politics). We have theology that offers healthy *priorities* in thinking about politics (that is, guidance for balancing legitimate political aspirations with needs in other areas of life). We have theology that could equip believers with healthy *attitudes* when acting politically (that is, guidance for how to regard the engagement with political problems, struggles, and outcomes). And we have a theology that in its biblical wisdom can help to ascertain healthy *political goals* (that is, guidance for determining what should be sought through political means). In a word, the history of Christian engagement in American politics shows the need for healthier motives, priorities, attitudes, and goals; Lutheran theology seems poised to meet that need.

It does so, first, because a genuinely Lutheran politics begins with the most important thing, not only for politics but for everything. And that most important thing is free justification before God, manifest to humanity in the redeeming work of Jesus Christ, and apprehended by faith. The best book that I know on Lutheran politics is Robert Benne's *The Paradoxical Vision*. It begins at exactly the right place:

The central paradox of the Christian faith is that God's salvation of the rebellious world is wrought through the life, death, and resurrection of an obscure Jewish figure, Jesus of Nazareth. . . . We are justified in God's grace through faith on account of Christ. . . . Justification by grace through faith on account of Christ is the glowing core of the Lutheran interpretation of the Christian gospel. Obviously such an interpretation is explicitly present in the New Testament and in the whole of the Christian tradition. It is not a Lutheran idiosyncrasy, but it is a Lutheran emphasis, thus holding up the radicality of God's grace.[1]

The second thing that Lutheranism offers grows from understanding what justification meant within the divine economy. It is Luther's theology of the cross, an understanding that he announced in the Ninety-Five Theses of 1517, expanded trenchantly at a dispute in Heidelberg only months later, and then returned to repeatedly throughout the rest of his life. The crucial element here is again a paradox: to understand the power that made heaven and earth it is necessary to know the powerlessness that hung on a Roman gibbet. To conceive the moral perfection of deity it is necessary to understand the scandal, the shame, the pain, and the sordidness of a criminal's execution. For Luther, in short, to find God was to find the cross.

What are the political implications of the strong Lutheran concentration on justification by grace through faith and on a theology of the cross?

First, since justification is God's work graciously offered to guilty sinners, it means that for anyone to be justified by faith is to recognize that only God has inalienable rights. Strictly considered, in Pascal's phrase, "God owes us nothing." Before God, who is the best and perfect arbiter, we do not deserve anything. All that we have — including the possibilities for wholesome political life — is a gift. Because of God's mercy, we and other humans do in fact have political rights, but only because they were bestowed upon us by a loving heavenly Father.

Second, to be justified by faith is never entirely to credit one's own motives for political action. By God's redeeming grace, believers may begin to act altruistically, and by his general grace so too in some circumstances may unbelievers. But because our need for God is so thorough, because we remain affected by sin even when are justified, it is only fitting to be properly cautious about ascribing too much righteousness to our own political action or too much perfidy to our political foes. "Why do you call me good? No one is good but God alone" (Luke 18:19).

Third, a strong doctrine of justification warns us that to succeed in political struggle is to confront new temptations for idolatry of self or of the political goal. It is a natural human tendency to invest great signifi-

---

1. Robert Benne, *The Paradoxical Vision: A Public Theology for the Twenty-first Century* (Minneapolis: Fortress, 1995), pp. 64-65.

cance in our own selves and also in the ideals, principles, traditions, or standards that mean the most to us. But precisely the best political goods can be the most dangerous to Christian believers if those goods ever come to supplant the supreme place in existence that belongs to God alone.

Finally, a fourth implication from these central Lutheran teachings is that to be victorious in Christ is to suffer with Christ. The ideal of American life that features so large in political rhetoric and consumerist culture is that things may one day be perfect here on earth — with just a few more votes, just a few more of the right products, just a little more money, just a little more security. It is a lie. To the extent that perfection exists on this earth, it is found only in the wounds of Christ.

The Lutheran principle of Two Kingdoms strikes me as a third much-needed contribution to contemporary thinking about Christianity and politics. As I understand this principle, it asserts that God has ordained the church to be, through word and sacrament, the human agency of eternal salvation and that he has ordained the state to be a guardian of public life for all people, both Christian believers and those who are not Christians. As I would put it, God's general love is shown to humanity by the protections provided for all in a well-functioning political sphere; his special love to humanity is shown by the provisions offered in and through the church for humans to be reconciled with himself. With this teaching goes the strong Lutheran emphasis on vocation. God's special calling to all humans is to repent and believe the gospel; but his general call to all humans is to be active in the terrestrial tasks that the hand finds to do. In both special and general callings, the end is the glory of God, which, however, might not be obvious in the broad sphere of the world, since not everyone there acknowledges that the world is created by God and that its potential for human flourishing is a gracious gift of God.

The political implications flowing from a Two Kingdoms theology, and an attendant concept of vocation, seem to me quite far-reaching (although I'll admit that at this point I may be ascribing to Luther's Two Kingdoms theology some of what actually comes from my own Calvinism as articulated by Abraham Kuyper).

First, God is the ruler over all, including the political sphere.

Second, political tasks are God-ordained; moreover, God himself has provided norms for discerning what is most important in the political sphere. If there were space, I think I could show from Scripture that the three most important norms, or mandates, for politics under God are the preservation of justice for all people, the special protection of the weak and marginal, and the imperative to treat all humans as image bearers of God.

Third, since God-ordained political tasks exist in a different sphere from God-ordained means of salvation, these political tasks may be carried out honorably by non-Christians as well as by Christians, and sometimes better by non-Christians than by Christians. One of the special strengths of Two Kingdoms theology is to detach the personal standing before God of political leaders from their political actions. Since believers continue to suffer the effects of sin and since nonbelievers have been given certain general human capacities by God, when it comes to life in the worldly sphere, it is entirely possible for nonbelievers to act politically with greater wisdom, fairness, and justice, than do believers. (The American civil rights movement is a great instance in American history where the liberal churches acted much better than their theology, while the theologically conservative churches acted much worse than their theology.)

Fourth, political callings offer Christian believers important avenues for service to God. Service to God in the political world is different than service to God in the church. But since God is Lord of the second sphere, as well as of the first, political service can still be genuine service to God.

Fifth, the priesthood of all believers (in the kingdom of Christ) implies that all humans, believers along with nonbelievers, possess (in the kingdom of the world) a potential for fruitful political service. I'm not sure how far I want to press this analogy, but it seems to suggest that documents like the United Nations' Universal Declaration of Human Rights deserve a great deal of support from Christian communities since such statements affirm what, by gift of the creation, God has ordained for all people.

A fourth foundation stone of Lutheran theology with a direct bearing on politics is the doctrine of *simul justus et peccator* — the believer is fully justified by God, through God's forensic redeeming action, but at the same time is still a sinner who will not exist with entire purity of motives and actions until perfected in the life to come. Of course, Lutherans hasten to say, we do also teach a doctrine of sanctification, which describes the growth in positive holiness that is normal for believers. But even a proper doctrine of sanctification should not lead Christians to think that they in themselves will ever be perfected in this life. Perfection is reserved for God alone.

At least two important implications for politics flow from *simul justus et peccator*. First, to know that truths can be held in tension with each other is to encourage political action marked by a certain reserve growing out of an awareness that multiple, apparently contradictory realities, may in fact be true about the same thing. Robert Benne has called this attitude "the paradoxical vision," while James Nuechterlein, among others, has spoken of it as "the Lutheran dialectic." Since we are talking about paradoxes here, the balance is hard to put into simple sentences. But certainly to be aware that the best political actions fall short of divine standards (there are none truly righteous but God), and that the worst political actions contain something human (because they too have been made possible by God and preserved by his providence) should be to promote a measure of humility about one's own political goals and behaviors; it should be to promote a self-critical perspective on all political evaluations and actions.

Second, Christian believers are free to attempt all in the political sphere, since they know they will never be able to achieve all in any sphere. That is, justification by faith, which some have seen leading to a passive quietism, should in reality be the most energizing force imaginable. If I am *not* trusting my actions in the political sphere to secure my redemption, but rather, if I see the possibility of righteous political action as a gift given to me (and all others) by a gracious God out of the mere goodness of his own heart, then as a Christian believer, I can be *ganz begeistert*, entirely enthusiastic, about taking part. I have been given a chance to help God; nothing depends ultimately on me.

Let me provide one concrete example for what a Lutheran perspective might mean in a concrete situation.[2] I happen to consider the fight against abortion on demand the noblest cause of the New Christian Right. Along with strong support for civil rights for the marginalized, it is one of the features of contemporary "Christian politics" that comes closest to fulfilling the biblical mandate to care for the powerless. While I do not agree with every tactical move or intellectual argument of the most visible pro-life leaders, I commend their work in general and often ask myself why I am not more active on behalf of expectant mothers and their children in utero. But I also happen to think that, as vitally important as the pro-life cause is, it is possible that those who sin in promoting abortion may yet be saved by

---

2. The next two paragraphs adapt material from Mark A. Noll, *Adding Cross to Crown: The Political Significance of Christ's Passion* (Grand Rapids: Baker, 1996), pp. 36-37. In this book there is a little more on why I think a Lutheran perspective could be greatly useful to political practice as a whole.

God's free grace in Christ, and that it is possible for pro-life advocates so thoroughly to commit themselves to their cause that they run the risk of trusting in their own pro-life advocacy as the sine qua non of their acceptance before God. I hope a fervent pro-life advocacy, which deals justly with both mothers- and children-to-be, will flourish, but I also hold that the political attitudes of those who think as I do will be more thoroughly Christian if we continue to remember that we are pro-life because we are Christians and not Christians because we are pro-life.

In general, it seems to me that Lutheran perspectives will do most good when they moderate Christian political attitudes in situations of conflict. There are, and always will be, culture wars. There are, and always will be, saints defending the truth and scoffers assaulting the truth. But for one who truly knows Christ, the culture wars will always be recognized for what they are — as *relatively* important battles, as warfare fought with *relatively* secure knowledge of who the enemy is and what the issues at stake are. The reason why the Christian who remembers Christ knows that culture wars can never be fought with more than relative certainty is the reason Alexander Solzhenitsyn spelled out with piercing clarity in *The Gulag Archipelago,* when he wrote, "If only [the struggle between good and evil] were so simple! If only there were evil people somewhere insidiously committing evil deeds, and it were necessary only to separate them from the rest of us and destroy them. But the line dividing good and evil cuts through the heart of every human being. And who is willing to destroy a piece of his own heart?"[3] In a word, there is a field of combat even more fundamental than the arena of public culture. That more fundamental field is the human heart where for every person, believer and unbeliever alike, the battle between God and self, light and dark, righteousness and corruption, is fought every day and where there will be no absolute, complete, or perfect triumph until the end of time. That, it seems to me, is a Lutheran statement.

*　　*　　*

So why, in American history, have Lutherans appeared to exert such scant positive effect on the course of political life? I can think of ten possible an-

---

3. Alexander Solzhenitsyn, *The Gulag Archipelago, 1918-1956* (English trans.; New York: Harper & Row, 1974), p. 168.

swers, which can be grouped into five general categories. Were I young and able to pick an important American subject for rigorous theological-historical investigation for an extended period, I would love to carry out the research required to validate or invalidate these hunches. But here I can present them only as possibilities.

Wrong Assumption

1. In fact, Lutherans have done much more good politically, and in a much broader terrain, than I am aware. This good may have been accomplished in unnoticed corners of the land (for example, Minnesota, South Dakota, certain parts of North Carolina) or through unsung Christian heroes (for example, Sen. Paul Simon or Bread for the World's Art Simon). If so, the premise of this essay is faulty.

Difficulties at the Source

2. Or maybe the theology of Luther that seems so propitious for political use was actually shown to be deficient by Luther's own inconsistent practice. When he justified heavy-handed political actions from Duke Frederick and other princely supporters of the Reformation as "bishops of necessity" *(Notbischöfe)*, or when he advocated civil penalties for Jews who would not convert to Christianity, maybe he was showing that it was simply impossible for political practice in the world of real-life dilemmas to live up to the beauty of his own theology. And if Luther could not do it, why should anyone expect later Lutherans to be able to live out the political potential of that theology?

3. Maybe Luther and later Lutherans never really believed what their own theology affirmed about vocation, since among Lutherans a theology of vocation has never become a spur for Christian service except among those who have pursued clerical vocations.

4. Perhaps the notorious quietism, whereby Lutherans in many different settings have chosen to remain on the political sidelines, is an inevitable outcome of a Two Kingdoms theology. In particular, where Two Kingdoms theology encourages a situation where the brightest young Lutherans are pointed toward vocations in the kingdom of Christ, and where little stress is placed on the importance of God-honoring service in the kingdom of the world, it seems inevitable that Lutheran politics would not live up to Lutheran theology.

New World Circumstances

5. But maybe the issue, rather, is that Lutheranism was a theology forged in the Old World, where assumptions of Christendom prevailed widely; in the New World, where Christendom is much weaker, Lutherans have always simply been out of their element.
6. Moreover, whatever their difficulties in the Old World, Lutheran communities in the New World may always have been simply too small and too dispersed to gain the critical mass required for effective political influence.
7. In addition, since early Lutherans in America were consumed by the internal needs characteristic of immigrant communities, and since later Lutherans have continued earlier patterns by concentrating on doing good for their own communities (hospitals, insurance, retirement, schools), there simply has never been the scope to develop an active Lutheran theology for the world as a whole.

Cultural Incomprehensibility

8. Orthodox Lutheranism has relied heavily upon certification for leadership based on formal higher education (in an America where authority more typically follows charisma). It has also self-consciously stressed traditionalism in music, foreign languages, and specialized theological vocabulary (in an America where almost no day-to-day communication takes place by relying on classical music, German or Latin, and a specialized theological vocabulary). Perhaps a result is that the forms of Lutheranism make it incomprehensible to almost all Americans, except those who have been raised Lutheran.

Spiritual Weakness

9. Maybe Lutheran ethnic and cultural tribalism has made it possible to keep Lutheran dogma alive, but at the expense of living piety. Yet only where living piety infuses dogma, however biblically sound that dogma is, can Christianity come to life as a dynamic social and political, as well as religious, force.
10. Lutherans may have been no less susceptible to spiritually enervating American fashions (for example, liberal individualism, atavistic anti-Romanism, all-or-nothing anti-communism, modern consumerism)

than believers in other Christian traditions. If so, it means that American Lutherans may have never really explored the political implications of their own theology.

*   *   *

The promise of a modest, discerning, careful, but also effective Christian politics seems to lie within the reach of those who have built their religious communities around the key theological insights of Martin Luther. Why that influence has not been forthcoming, or has been forthcoming only intermittently, remains to me a mystery. Because the rest of American Christianity so badly needs what Lutheran theology seems to offer, God hasten the day when the Lutheran potential is actualized as a positive Christian force.

CONTESTED ISSUES IN PUBLIC THEOLOGY

Luther and Liberalism

PAUL R. HINLICKY

As Professor Benne is a political *liberal*[1] as well as a theological *Lutheran*,[2] it is fitting to offer an essay on the theme entitled above in celebration of the happy occasion of his seventieth birthday and in commemoration of his many fruitful years of service as a Christian ethicist and public theologian.

Luther's recent biographer, Martin Brecht, called attention to philosopher Herbert Marcuse's attack on Luther for "limiting the concern of freedom to the inward man and thus with diverting the Germans from their true needs for freedom."[3] Marcuse's critique stems woodenly from the early Marx: "Luther, to be sure, vanquished the bondage of devotion when he replaced it with the bondage of conviction. He shattered faith in authority while he restored the authority of faith. He transformed parsons into laymen and laymen into parsons. He freed man from outward religiosity while he made religiosity the innerness of men. He emancipated the body from its chain while he puts chains on the heart."[4] To this criticism Brecht responds: It "begs the fundamental question of how freedom is to be achieved. Lu-

---

1. "Liberal" in the classic not contemporary, popular sense. I would like to acknowledge my own debt to Benne's seminal work, *The Ethics of Democratic Capitalism: A Moral Reassessment* (Philadelphia: Fortress, 1981).

2. Among many publications, see Benne's particularly "Lutheran" studies *Ordinary Saints: An Introduction to the Christian Life* (Philadelphia: Fortress, 1988); and *The Paradoxical Vision: A Public Theology for the Twenty-first Century* (Minneapolis: Fortress, 1995).

3. Martin Brecht, *Martin Luther: His Road to Reformation, 1483-1521*, trans. J. L. Schaf (Minneapolis: Fortress, 1993), p. 409.

4. Karl Marx, *On Religion*, ed. S. K. Padover (New York: McGraw-Hill, 1974), pp. 36-37.

ther's answer was: by liberation as a gift, not through activistic self-realization." Of course, a gift presupposes a Giver: real freedom consists in humanity's "election to communion with God." This of course *is* a scandal to modern sensibilities, but *not only* to modern ones. Brecht rightly notes: "This understanding was just as contrary to the conventional view of man at [Luther's] time as it is to the modern views of human possibilities."[5]

Eberhard Jüngel has also rejoined the Marx-Marcuse line. Luther in his great treatise, *The Freedom of the Christian*, Jüngel writes, "asserts first of all that the *inner man*, in total contrast to an 'I' shut up in its 'inwardness,' can allow *himself to be called out of himself* and can actually *come out of himself* so as to become a new man."[6] We can be set free from self and become free for others because God is there in the gospel calling us out of ourselves to the *glorious liberty of the children of God* (Romans 8), promising that *we shall be changed* (1 Corinthians 15). For Luther, in faith already now this future of freedom is anticipated as a kind of *rapture* or *ecstasy*. Faith lives outside the self, rejoicing in God's favor and at the same time in the same love descending to the neighbor in need. This rapture or ecstasy of faith is the beginning of *true* freedom, *from* self and *for* God and others. The sticking point is that such change is something that happens to us, something given to us through the call of God in the gospel, in the promise that takes present hold in faith. Thus, for Luther this true freedom is radically, exclusively theological — and so for Marx and Marcuse and many others like them illusory.

If it is not an illusion, if this *change* from bondage to freedom is a reality, Jüngel writes following Luther's famous statement against Erasmus, it is because an *exchange* occurs in faith. Freedom properly is "an exclusively divine predicate,"[7] not ours by nature,[8] but only by grace, as gift, and so *mediated*. In Luther's motif of the *joyful exchange* that transpires between Christ and the believer, Christ takes away sin and death and gives in their place his righteousness and life. The royal freedom of the king and representative offering of great high priest becomes the believer's by grace.[9] "Lords of all subject to none": freed from all the idols and demons that tor-

---

5. Brecht, *Martin Luther*, p. 409.

6. Eberhard Jüngel, *The Freedom of a Christian: Luther's Significance for Contemporary Theology*, trans. R. A. Harrisville (Minneapolis: Augsburg, 1988), p. 63.

7. Jüngel, *The Freedom of a Christian*, p. 69.

8. Jüngel, *The Freedom of a Christian*, pp. 19-27.

9. Jüngel, *The Freedom of a Christian*, pp. 70-87.

ment lost humanity; "servants of all subject to everyone": freed in service to others by the agape love that Christ the servant Lord first brought to us. This in a word is what Luther has to say about freedom: we are not free but in bondage. We are freed; we become free when God in Christ makes us his own.

What has this exclusively theological event to do with the struggle today for human freedom in the world? There have been many, mutually incompatible attempts to assert the relevance of Luther for modern people seeking freedom, just as there are also many conflicting assessments of freedom. I want to sort our way through some of these disputes. The goal is to put the theological Luther for whom freedom is the event of divine liberation in the joyful exchange of Christ and faith into conversation with contemporary political liberalism. Fifteen years ago an American philosopher very foolishly proclaimed that with the fall of communism, the "end of history" had come in the sense that all alternatives to liberalism had collapsed. But today liberalism is again very much in doubt. It is threatened from within by what Reinhold Niebuhr identified in the 1930s as the "naïve cynicism" of moralists and idealists who do not see with Christian realism the moral ambiguity of *any* conceivable exercise of political power in a fallen world and thus the necessity of making hard choices amid greater and lesser evils. Today political liberalism is again confronted from without by powerful critiques of liberty in the name of equality and fraternity, i.e., the rival ideologies which once went by the names of communism and fascism. Names have changed but the ideologies remain. The present effort in Lutheran theology is critically to affirm liberalism as the way between the Scylla and Charybdis of those totalizing modern ideologies.

Pitfalls in the Theme of Luther's Relevance

How is Luther relevant to the cause of liberty in the modern world? What is the relation between the celebrated freedom of the modern world and Martin Luther? The question is hardly new; it has been hotly debated since the American and French revolutions at the turn of the eighteenth century. This debate has witnessed the most varied hypotheses. Traditional Lutherans still remember Luther as the father of their separated church, a memory filtered through the theology of Melanchthon and the post-Reformation polemics of the century-long wars of religion. For many of these traditional Lutherans, Luther is their revered Moses who led them out from the bondage of medieval superstition and papal tyranny. For the early modern liberal, on the other hand, Luther is remembered as the hero of individual conscience who defied the Emperor at the Diet of Worms and set European culture on the path to the separation of church and state and religious tolerance. For the Enlightenment, Luther is the first man who had the courage to think for himself, free from the hallowed prejudice of the past, testing all claims and holding only to what stood the test of Reason. For nineteenth-century Romantics, Luther was the shining beacon of awakening national consciousness, who liberated Germans and their language from Mediterranean cultural superiority. In the realm of modern theology, Luther became for Albrecht Ritschl and his school the discoverer of the simple truth of the loving God, a new image which delivered from medieval superstition about the wrath of God.[10] In the so-called Luther Renaissance of Karl Holl in the Germany of the 1920s, Luther became the "German Saviour," whose religious personality could rally the defeated and discouraged Germans.[11] In the 1930s Luther became for *die deutsche Christen* the religious champion of German liberation from international Jewry.[12]

In all this dubious hero worship of Luther, it is essential to recall that Luther is remembered quite differently in other circles. Jews have remembered him as one who called for synagogues to be burned and the people driven out of the land. The proletariat has remembered him as one who

10. "Ritschl rejected the notion of God's wrath as fundamentally at odds with Luther's anti-juristic outlook, and thus saw it as a relapse into an Anselmic mode of thinking." David Lotz, *Ritschl and Luther: A Fresh Perspective on Albrecht Ritschl's Theology in the Light of His Luther Study* (Nashville: Abingdon, 1974), p. 154.

11. Cf., inter alia, John Dillenberger, *God Hidden and Revealed: The Interpretation of Luther's Deus Absconditus and Its Significance for Religious Thought* (Philadelphia: Muhlenberg, 1953); James M. Stayer, *Martin Luther, German Saviour: German Evangelical Theological Factions and the Interpretation of Luther, 1917-1933* (Montreal: McGill-Queens University Press, 2000).

12. None less than Nazi ideologue Alfred Rosenberg published a book, *Protestant Pilgrims to Rome: The Treason against Luther,* which argued that the confessing church was "slowly moving back in the direction of St. Peter. Ignatius Loyola, not Martin Luther, was now being made head of German Protestantism. . . . Sterile dogmatism and clerical infantilism were replacing Luther's fiery spirit of protest 'against Rome and Jerusalem.'" Richard Steigmann-Gall, *The Holy Reich: Nazi Conceptions of Christianity 1919-1945* (Cambridge: Cambridge University Press, 2003), p. 128.

counseled princes to slaughter uprising peasants with a good conscience fulfilling their duty to the Lord. Roman Catholics have remembered Luther not as a liberal but as a libertine who could not discipline his own passions and so unleashed a flood of hedonism, greed, and irreligion which destroyed the unity of the church. All these memories have a grain of truth in them. The attempt to make a hero for modernity out of the historical Martin Luther, it seems to me, is full of pitfalls.

The most influential debate in scholarly circles about this began almost one hundred years ago. Liberal theology's greatest representative, Ernst Troeltsch, argued that Luther is so thoroughly a medieval thinker that his theology and ethic are a version of the medieval synthesis of church and state. In other words, Luther sought to reform and renew the Constantinian system. He can therefore have no more than historical meaning for us today who on account of the principle of freedom of conscience reject the political idea that any church can or should play a culturally hegemonic role. It is "simply the medieval idea of the *Corpus Christianum,* within which, in the modern sense of the word, there is, as yet, no separation between Church and State, between sacred and secular. The civil authority and the ecclesiastical authority are two different aspects of the one undivided Christian Society, for which reason the Government and the State have directly Christian aims, and the Church includes the whole of Society."[13] In this forthright call for the disestablishment of the Christian church in European culture, Troeltsch was following the lead of Immanuel Kant, the great philosopher of the Enlightenment and also a nominal Lutheran. In his influential treatise, *Religion within the Limits of Reason Alone,* Kant argued that with the progress of reason comes freedom from dogma, which dissolves under the acid of criticism. Thus, the ecclesiastical form of faith, under the tutelage of the state, must also dissolve and be replaced by civil society building the kingdom of God on earth. Kant's vision of the end of the church and its assimilation into modern society defined the debate for the century to follow, up through the First World War and Troeltsch's theology.

Karl Holl rose up against Troeltsch. He was a fellow liberal and also follower of Kant, but deeply stricken by the crisis of Kant's project for a modern society wrought by the devastation of the Great War. Holl held

13. Ernst Troeltsch, *The Social Teachings of the Christian Churches,* vol. 2, trans. O. Wyon (New York: Harper Torchbooks, 1961), p. 522.

that the modern world had originated in Luther's revolt against Rome and that the modern world could only rediscover its spiritual basis and recover its orientation by a return to Luther — really to Luther's heroic personal faith, *not* to his dogmatic theology. For Holl, the great thing about Luther's personal faith was that it was "ethical," that is, not superstitious, magical, manipulative, self-serving but a genuine freedom from self for God and others. Thus the so-called Luther Renaissance was born. Holl and his students issued a series of first rate scholarly studies of Luther's vast corpus under the assumption that Luther, properly delivered by historical critical methods from the remnants of medieval superstition, could still inspire modern people to a public faith in the forgiving love of God as a resource for ethical living, thereby securing humanist values and fostering European renewal.

Holl put the question this way: "What do people really look for in religion? Does religion involve a relationship to an Absolute above and beyond oneself, or is it really only a relationship to oneself, to one's own metaphysical ground of being? Is the Ultimate around which religion revolves hidden from us in impenetrable darkness so that the only possibility is a 'silent veneration,' a religion 'as if,' perhaps even a 'religion without God?' Or is it possible for us to approach the deepest mystery, and is there a duty to do so? Is religion, viewed historically, only a carry over from our most primitive stage, a tenaciously maintained residue of prescientific thinking, or is it something that transcends all mere rationality, the concealed motive force for the whole higher development of humanity?" Holl took the position that religion involves a relation to the Absolute, whom we can and indeed must approach. Indeed, this quest for the Absolute is "the concealed motive force" of human progress — a progress, as I mentioned, now in crisis because of the Great War.

Approached this way, Luther is made a representative of a generally human-religious quest for the Absolute. "We do Luther no violence when we try to relate him to these questions. One side of him, it is true, is not at all amenable to this whole approach." That is, we redeem what is valuable in Luther by making him a representative of the generally human-religious quest for the Absolute, and in the process we purge him of what is accidental to his real genius and uncongenial to our sensibilities. What side of Luther is thus to be purged and left behind? This is the Luther who "recognized only one true religion . . . expressed in certain definite statements of faith, transmitted and preserved in a church," i.e., Kant's ecclesiastical form of faith. Despite such remnants of Catholicism in Luther, Holl argued that "Luther rebuilt from the ground up" by reconceiving God in ethical terms and so "gained his own personal conception of the Christian religion only in a controversy with the Catholic church."[14]

The result of this process, unsurprisingly, is a thoroughly modernized Luther, unrecognizable historically, recast in Holl's image as the pioneer of liberal religion. John Dillenberger, an American scholar of a half a century ago, described Holl's modernized Luther image this way: "Man, simply because of his limited nature, cannot see the full wonder of God in the world. At most there is the mystery of a God who loves one more than one knows and whose wrath one need not fear. . . . Jesus Christ is the revealer of God. What he reveals is that God will pardon man from his guilt, thereby releasing him for his work in the world. Through this one is elevated as a spiritual and moral person above the world and therefore into fellowship and communion with God."[15] All these features are characteristic of nineteenth-century liberal theology, for which science's uncovering of the natural world threatened to overwhelm human moral purposes and drag human beings down to the behavior of the beasts. In this climate, Luther becomes the discoverer of a divine grace that is not so much opposed to sin (which is forgiven by effortless fiat), nor to the wrath of God (which is ignored, if not discounted), but to vast impersonal nature working blindly and relentlessly.

In this modernized Luther, Jesus is central — but not because of "the unheard miracle of forgiveness in Jesus Christ."[16] Rather, Schleiermacher's Christ is projected back onto Luther: Jesus becomes the man perfectly conscious of the loving God, thus God's human revealer — though not himself the revealed Son of God in the flesh who pays the dear price of forgiveness at the cross and so overcomes the wrath of God, as thought the medieval Luther. Neither is God the mysterious Holy Trinity, nor is faith the rapture in the Holy Spirit. God is the kindly Father of lights, presiding over a universal brotherhood of man; faith is the human decision to believe in one's own moral worth, as revealed by Brother Jesus. The Christian calling is to be a good secular person, building the kingdom of God — *not the church!* — on the earth in a moral society, where each human being is

---

14. Karl Holl, *What Did Luther Understand by Religion?* trans. F. W. Meuser and W. R. Wietzke (Philadelphia: Fortress, 1977), p. 16.

15. Dillenberger, *God Hidden and Revealed*, p. 34.

16. Dillenberger, *God Hidden and Revealed*, p. 34.

treated as a person, an end, never as an instrument, a means. Jesus with Luther his best interpreter turns out to be the very best liberal!

I have gone on in some detail about the modernized Luther image created by Karl Holl and his followers to underscore an important point. Even though Holl captures freedom from self for God and others as central in his approach, we no longer recognize the historical Martin Luther in his modernizing portrait. In the process, everything interesting Luther might have to say to us today about human bondage and divine liberation has been washed out of the picture. Troeltsch has the greater historical right in this argument with Holl. Luther simply cannot be recast as the spiritual father of the modern world and its liberal theology without violence to history. Luther's real legacy is *problematic* in important respects. His attacks on Pope, peasants, and Jews as minions of Satan, to mention the most disturbing aspect, betray a superstitious belief in the devil that gave the historical Luther psychological permission to lash out in verbal violence against opponents.[17] Grotesquely there are Lutherans still today who think themselves the most faithful of all when they monkey this vile behavior. In reality we cannot today appropriate Luther's demonizing rhetoric and must rather repudiate it decisively if we are to have any chance at learning anything of theological value from the sixteenth-century reformer. Heaven help us, we don't need Luther to help us demonize opponents! By the same token, we can no longer resort to the convenient device of sweeping under the rug this or that unsavory notion we find in Luther with the simplistic smear that it is a "remnant of Catholicism or of medieval superstition." As the theological liberal Troeltsch knew, also the Incarnation, the Trinity, with all the other mysteries of faith including the canon of Holy Scripture are part and parcel "remnants of Catholicism" which are also swept away

---

17. Mark U. Edwards Jr. has located Luther's verbal violence against peasant, Pope, Turk, and Jew in his apocalyptic worldview. See "Luther's Polemical Controversies," in *The Cambridge Companion to Martin Luther*, ed. D. K. McKim (Cambridge: Cambridge University Press, 2003), p. 194. "Luther understood his disagreement with [opponents] in the context of this struggle between God and Satan. Behind them all loomed the figure of the devil, the father of lies. Often Luther directed his attacks not at his human opponents but at the devil whom he saw as their master, and, of course, no language was too harsh when attacking the devil" (p. 195). See also "Supermus: Luther's Own Fanatics," in *Seven-Headed Luther: Essays in Commemoration of a Quincentenary, 1483-1983*, ed. P. N. Brooks (Gloucestershire: Clarendon, 1983), pp. 123-46; *Luther's Last Battles: Politics and Polemics, 1531-46* (Ithaca, NY: Cornell University Press, 1983).

when we use such a big broom. Luther's theological understanding that true freedom is an event that comes upon us from without, a divine liberation for beings in bondage — this is most centrally what Luther has to say to us today about freedom and it is what most directly challenges contemporary sensibilities.

The Perils of Liberalism

But what, on the other hand, is liberalism? I take it that liberalism is a species of modernism, one of its forms of political economy. Since 1989 it has appeared as the predominant one, so far as free market economics and democratic polities have advanced. Yet here too we find a wide variety of theses, so that one man's liberalism is another's conservatism (or worse). The word "liberalism" derives from the Latin *libertas,* the freedom of a released slave; as a political philosophy, liberalism is that set of convictions about the organization of modern society which seeks to maximize the freedom of individuals and limit concentrations of power, especially, of the modern State. It is important, I think, to recall that liberalism is only one of several possible forms of modern political philosophy. If we take the threefold slogan of the French Revolution, *liberty, equality, fraternity* as guide to the quintessentially modern values, it is easy to see how liberalism takes up liberty and makes it the leading value in preference to the other two. In comparison, Marxism took up the value of equality and fascism the value of fraternity as guiding motives respectively. These three great modern political values have vied for dominance since the French Revolution. The legacy of none is without blemish, so much so that whatever else today's skeptical mood of so-called post-modernism may indicate, it is kind of a disgust and disillusionment with the grand dramatic political dreams of liberty, equality, fraternity in whose name so much blood has been shed in the past two centuries. One might think that the trick is to put the three values back together, as social democracy in Europe tries to do. But the tensions among these values are real. Any case for liberalism, I think, demands sober recognition of why this is so.

Dietrich Bonhoeffer analyzed the problem this way: "The American democracy is not founded upon the emancipated man but, quite the contrary, upon the kingdom of God and the limitation of all earthly powers by the sovereignty of God. It is indeed significant when, in contrast to the

[French Revolution's] *Declaration of the Rights of Man,* American historians can say that the federal constitution was written by men who were conscious of original sin and the wickedness of the human heart. Earthly wielders of authority, and also the people, are directed into their proper bounds, in due consideration of man's innate longing for power and of the fact that power pertains only to God."[18] Bonhoeffer has in mind Anglo-American thinkers like John Locke,[19] James Madison, and Abraham Lincoln,[20] all in the Calvinist tradition, whose liberalism was profoundly informed by the need to constrain human depravity in humble acknowledgement of divine sovereignty. For them, liberty comes, as Mary sings in the Magnificat, when in the course of human events the sovereign God "casts down the mighty from their thrones and exalts them of low degree" (Luke 1).

Put more mundanely: liberalism as a political philosophy is based upon bitter providential lessons about the tendency of political power to oppress those it pretends to serve and protect, especially under the banner of those other important values of equality and fraternity. When Stalin decided to starve the Kulaks in Ukraine in order to collectivize agriculture and smash the power of traditional farming communities, he is said to have cited the precedent of Napoleon Bonaparte: "We will drive the people to happiness with an iron fist!"[21] When Lincoln refused to support the immediate, violent end to the slave system advocated by the abolitionists, and worked instead for a gradual political and economic solution, it was because he rejected Bonapartism.[22] The roots of liberalism of course lie

18. Dietrich Bonhoeffer, *Ethics,* ed. E. Bethge (New York: Macmillan Paperback Edition, 1975), pp. 102, 104.

19. On Locke, see Paul R. Hinlicky, "The Future of Tolerance," in *All Theology Is Christology: Essays in Honor of David P. Scaer,* ed. Dean O. Wenthe et al. (Fort Wayne, IN: Concordia Theological Seminary Press, 2000), pp. 375-89.

20. See Paul R. Hinlicky, "Lincoln's Theology of the Republic According to the Second Inaugural Address," *The Cresset* 65, no. 6 (May 2002): 7-14.

21. Alan Bullock, *Hitler and Stalin: Parallel Lives* (New York: Alfred A. Knopf, 1992), pp. 272-324. Also, Stephen Lukes, *Marxism and Reality* (Oxford: Oxford University Press, 1987), pp. 100-138.

22. Harry V. Jaffa, *A New Birth of Freedom: Abraham Lincoln and the Coming of the Civil War* (Lanham, MD: Rowman & Littlefield, 2000), p. 116. Again Bonhoeffer: "The emancipation of the masses leads to the reign of terror and guillotine. Nationalism leads inevitably to war. The liberation of man as an absolute ideal leads only to man's self-destruction. At the end of the path which was first trodden in the French Revolution there is nihilism. The new unity which the French Revolution brought to Europe — and what we are

deeper in history than reaction against the disastrous precedent set by Napoleon's campaign to spread the blessings of the revolution by force. Just a decade or so before Napoleon, the English liberal Edmund Burke in his *Reflections on the Revolution in France* had prophesied the coming bloodshed unleashed by the Jacobin reign of terror. Burke had supported the American Revolution against the British crown; ironically today he is remembered as the father of "conservatism" in Anglo-American history. This is quite confused,[23] since Burke distrusted the paternalistic claims of the revolution for the same reason he distrusted the paternalistic claims of the crown. Burke in other words distrusted paternalism. He had learned this distrust of political power pretending to be our loving Father from John Locke, one of many early modern thinkers struggling to deliver Europe from the grip of the religious wars unleashed after the Reformation and to re-establish public life on a surer, more scientific basis than competing claims of Protestants and Catholics to divine authority. Locke is principally remembered for his theory that all knowledge derives from the individual's sensory experience, a theory which undergirds the liberal belief that nothing is to be taken on authority that cannot be tested in one's own experience.

But Locke's influential *Second Treatise of Government* argued in quite a different way than just mentioned. It is ostensibly directed against "the divine right of kings" theory of the monarchists but more interestingly it can be read as directed "between the lines" against a fellow modernist of the previous generation, Thomas Hobbes.[24] Hobbes's solution to the anarchy of religious war raging in England was the social contract theory: warring individuals abandon the miserable state of nature by banding together for collective security and ceding the sword to an absolute sovereign. Thus we pass from the state of nature to civil society. Hobbes thus presupposed a state of nature in which individuals driven by the natural law of self-preservation do all for gain or glory. He was able in this way to depict hu-

---

experiencing today in the crisis of this unity [i.e. under Hitlerism] — is therefore western godlessness . . . not the theoretical denial of the existence of God. It is itself a religion, a religion of hostility to God." Bonhoeffer, *Ethics,* p. 104.

23. No less a "progressive" than Jonathan Schell in his anti-nuclear treatise, *The Fate of the Earth,* invokes Burke's "covenant of the generations" as the fulcrum of moral responsibility. See Jonathan Schell, *The Fate of the Earth* (New York: Alfred A. Knopf, 1982).

24. Nicholas Jolley, *Locke: His Philosophical Thought* (Oxford and New York: Oxford University Press, 1999), p. 196.

man progress as an advance from a brutal state of nature to civil peace. There comes a point in the *bellum omnes contra omnem* when, led by the same law of self-preservation seeking gain and glory, we recognize the advantages of peace. Human beings are not, the Hobbesian claims, fallen angels but rising beasts. Progress comes by the mechanism of enlightened self-interest.

There is a cost, however. The price we pay for the advantages of peace and social progress is the modern emergence of *Leviathan,* as he named his book after the biblical sea-monster: a metaphor for a king or absolute dictator reigning as a god on the earth. *Leviathan* is the first theory of modern totalitarianism; it is also a work of (anti-)theology, specifically, a radically anti-Augustinian case for the city of man against the city of God, the church. Thus *Leviathan* labors to turn upside down the biblical narrative of creation and fall, as I mentioned: no longer are we fallen sinners redeemed in Christ. Now we are beasts rising by enlightened self-interest to civilized existence. In the process, Hobbes's scheme makes human community something unnatural, artificial, conventional, and contractual, even as the *Leviathan* of the totalizing secular state is in turn made necessary to fend off the war of all against all. It is crucial to see then how Hobbes ignored forms of community life in the antecedent state of nature: marriage, family or tribe, forms of common economic life like hunting, gathering, and agriculture (rather than rape and pillage) based on the bounty of the earth, and forms of common religious life expressed in gratitude and respect for life as the property of the common Creator, as we might read in the Bible and its interpreters.[25] But Hobbes writes: "in the state of mere nature . . . there are supposed no laws of matrimony, no laws for the education of children, but the law of nature, and the natural inclination of the sexes, one to another, and to their children."[26]

---

25. The *Ought* of duty is grounded in the *Is* of community. This interpretation of natural law lies at the font of Western, Latin civilization; in the words of Lactantius (250-330 CE), the "Christian Cicero" who tutored the children of Constantine: "Therefore kindness is the greatest bond of human society; and he who has broken this is to be deemed impious, and a parricide. For if we all derive our origin from one man, whom God created, we are plainly of one blood; and therefore, it must be considered the greatest wickedness to hate a man, *even though guilty.*" Lactantius, *The Divine Institutes* 6:10, trans. W. Fletcher, *The Ante-Nicene Fathers,* vol. 7, emphasis added.

26. Thomas Hobbes, *Leviathan,* with selected variants from the Latin edition of 1668, ed. E. M. Curley (Indianapolis: Hackett, 1994), p. 129.

Locke restored just these missing elements of community life to his account of the state of nature: "Paternal or parental power is nothing but that which parents have over their children, to govern them for the children's good, till they come to the use of reason . . . [and] live as freemen. . . . The affection and tenderness which God hath planted in the breast of parents toward their children, makes it evident, that this is not intended to be a severe arbitrary government, but only for the help, instruction and preservation of their offspring. . . . [T]he paternal is a natural government," which terminates when the child becomes an adult.[27] What difference does this account of community in the state of nature make? Locke in short will not need a paternal state — really a dictatorship pretending to care for us as did Papa Stalin — because God has already established parenthood in the state of nature. Consequently, he argued that only limited rights connected with security were ceded to the sovereign in the social contract; the people retain to themselves all other natural rights of family, economy, and religion. Should the social covenant be broken, i.e., should the state fail to maintain peace or protect natural rights, the people retain the right of what Locke called, after the Bible, "an appeal to heaven," i.e., the right to armed revolt. (This is the thinking on the right to revolution which stands behind the American Declaration of Independence.) Locke in these ways sought to retrieve the biblical account of a fall from the peace of Paradise and exile into the wilderness of sin, waiting for the coming of a true Prince of Peace, the Messiah of the Lord; in the meantime, the power of the sword is fraught with moral ambiguity, at once necessary yet full of danger: it must constrain the sinner — yet those who constrain are themselves also sinners. This sober biblical realism recognizes that the state, any state, even the democratic state, is as such a monopoly of coercive power, both necessary (Romans 13) and dangerous (Revelation 13).

In America, it was Reinhold Niebuhr in the middle of the last century, along with his conversation partner from Germany, the previously cited Dietrich Bonhoeffer, who more than any other modern Lutheran[28] retrieved

27. John Locke, *Second Treatise of Government*, ed. C. B. Macpherson (Indianapolis: Hackett, 1980), pp. 88-89.

28. Niebuhr was a member of the Union church, the German Evangelical and Reformed Synod. Although he frequently criticized Luther's conservatism, quietism, and paternalism along the lines of Troeltsch's critique, which he often uncritically relied on, in his theological appropriation of freedom as forgiveness and renewal given by God, he is "Lutheran" in the sense that this lecture deems relevant.

Locke's suspicion and critique of state paternalism with the Christian doctrine of original sin. The state is necessary because: (1) the sinful temptation
to exalt oneself at the expense of others infects all people; (2) as a matter of
conscience (Rom. 13:5) this universal propensity of pride to resort to violence must be forcibly as well as lawfully constrained. Yet the State is dangerous, because the state which enforces this minimum of justice on behalf of
God is itself populated by self-interested sinners, who find it all too easy to
rationalize oppression of others, when they tell themselves that it is for their
own good. In a classical discussion of the self-deceptions of collective egoism on the level of the modern state, Niebuhr put it this way: "Nations may
fight for 'liberty' and 'democracy' but they do not do so until their vital interests are imperiled. They may refuse to fight and claim that their refusal is
prompted by their desire to 'preserve civilization.' Neutral nations are not
less sinful than belligerent ones in their effort to hide their partial interests
behind their devotion to 'civilization.' . . . This does not mean that men may
not have to make fateful decisions between types of civilization in mortal
combat. The moralists who contend that the imperfections of all civiliza-
tions negate every obligation to preserve any of them suffer from a naïve
cynicism. Relative distinctions must always be made in history [even
though] the collective life of man . . . is invariably involved in the sin of
pride."[29] Thus there must be a coercive state in a fallen and sinful world to
curb violence; at the same time, the state must be held in check by popular
sovereignty and a constitutional law based upon inviolable civil liberties.
Thus in liberalism *liberty is secured as the minimum basis* for civilized life
and the prospect of progress on the other values of equality and fraternity.

Let us frankly acknowledge what this decision for the primacy of civil
liberty means. The liberal state does not as such secure the values either of
equality or fraternity. It leaves a value like fraternity to other forms of association than the state, and indeed rejects as fascist any call to forge an or-
ganic society backed by the coercive power of the state. Like Lincoln, it
leaves even a value like equality to social evolution through the democratic
political process. The American Revolution left the morally abhorrent inequality of the slave system intact (in the case of Thomas Jefferson against
his own conscience),[30] for the most part blinded to this evil by the collec-

29. Reinhold Niebuhr, *The Nature and Destiny of Man*, vol. 1 (New York: Charles
Scribner's Sons, 1941), pp. 213-14.

30. "[King George] has waged cruel war against human nature itself, violating its most

tive egoism of white racism. It took the breakdown of civil war and then another century of social struggle to advance that cause of human equality. Marxist opponents of liberalism have always been able to attack the hypocrisy of bourgeois liberty for such grievous failures; but the liberal way in turn rejects Marxist or fascist Bonapartism. Self-governing people have themselves to change and be changed by the process of democratic debate and political decision in all its sharpness and confusion and sometimes even breakdown, if values like equality and forms of fraternal community are to advance and evolve. When the American Revolution institutionally separated church and state, it left the pursuit of happiness and the formation of fraternal community to individual decision and voluntary association. The liberal public is cold *Gesellschaft,* not warm *Gemeinschaft,* and this gives the impression today of Western godlessness, especially in the eyes of Islam.[31] Attacks on liberal democracy have always been able to point to the anomie, the fragmentation and isolation experienced under liberalism.[32] The liberal way rejects the false promise of solidarity. Under liberalism people must find fraternity in communities *disarmed,* lest holy war, crusade, and/or jihad resume and we all return to the darkness of those wars of religion out of which liberalism emerged.

---

sacred rights of life and liberty in the persons of a distant people who never offended him, captivating and carrying them into slavery in another hemisphere, or to incur miserable death in their transportation hither. This piratical warfare, the opprobrium of INFIDEL powers, is the warfare of the CHRISTIAN king of Great Britain. Determined to keep open a market where MEN should be bought and sold, he has prostituted his negative for suppressing every legislative attempt to prohibit or to restrain this execrable commerce. . . ." Jefferson's Draft of the Declaration excised by the Constitutional Assembly, in *The Portable Thomas Jefferson,* ed. Merrill D. Peterson (New York: Penguin Books, 1977), p. 239.

31. In May of 2006, for recent example, Iranian President Mahmoud Ahmadinejad wrote an open letter to U.S. President Bush. It is in many ways a poignant case for progress on social equality in the world that many of us would endorse. But his case turns on the loss of fraternity in liberal societies: "The people of many countries are angry about the attacks on their cultural foundations and the disintegration of families. They are equally dismayed with the fading of care and compassion. . . . Liberalism and Western style democracy have not been able to help realize the ideals of humanity. Today these two concepts have failed. Those with insight can already hear the sounds of the shattering and fall of the ideology and thoughts of the Liberal democratic systems." So Ahmadinejad's letter concludes with a summons to Islamic revolution, which will restore the lost fraternity.

32. As Max Weber analyzed so presciently in his 1919 lecture "Politics as Vocation." Max Weber, "Politik als Beruf," in *Gesammelte Politische Schriften* (Munich: Dunker & Humboldt, 1919); now available in English translation on *Wikipedia.*

Conclusion

All the same, we are spiritually dying in the West today for lack of fraternity, *Gemeinschaft*, solidarity, what Josiah Royce once named the "Beloved
Community."[33] In so far as we are and must be liberals who patiently work
for greater equality in society, however, we must recognize that we cannot
get fraternity from politics and we must be deeply suspicious of those who
so desire. Liberal politics can and must work for greater equality but cannot claim fraternity without jeopardizing the freedom of conscience, the
freedom to criticize, the freedom of dissent, the freedom of association.
We have to embrace this dilemma. If we do that, I submit, we might learn
again from Martin Luther that *the church* in gospel essence *is* and *ought to
become again* amid these ruins the brotherhood-sisterhood, the fraternity-
sorority, the *Gemeinschaft*, the holy community of those crying out for the
glorious liberty of the children of God *because* in Christ they have already
now been *changed*, really *ex-changed* to faith: "I believe that there is on this
earth a holy little flock and community of pure saints under one head,
Christ. It is called together by the Holy Spirit in one faith, mind, and understanding. It possesses a variety of gifts, and yet is united in love without
sect or schism. Of this community I also am a part and member, a participant and co-partner in all the blessings it possesses."[34] The *event* on the
earth of divine liberation from bondage to self communicated in the gospel takes place as this *communio*, or it does not take place at all.

33. Josiah Royce, *The Problem of Christianity* (Washington, DC: Catholic University of
America Press, 2001), pp. 75-98.
34. "The Large Catechism," in *The Book of Concord*, ed. Charles P. Arand, Timothy J.
Wengert, Robert Kolb (Minneapolis: Augsburg Fortress, 2000), pp. 437-38.

The Public Theologian as Connected Critic: The Case of Central European Churches

Ronald F. Thiemann

As I write this essay, the United States, the world's oldest liberal democracy and its sole military superpower, is mired in a fifth year of combat in Iraq. Despite strong criticism by religious leaders and communities, despite widespread opposition within the international community, and despite only modest support from the American public, the Bush administration invaded Iraq, arguing that American safety was threatened by the presence of "weapons of mass destruction" and the growing likelihood of Iraq's nuclear capability.[1] These arguments were soon shown to be based upon

---

1. My Harvard colleague, David Little, has documented this trend in an as yet unpublished paper entitled "Terrorism, Public Emergency, and International Order: The U.S. Example." Especially distressing is the content of the National Security Strategy Document issued September 17, 2002, that asserts, "While the US will constantly strive to enlist the support of the international community, we will not hesitate to act alone, if necessary, to exercise our right of self-defense by acting preemptively." Little worries that the appeal to the language of "emergency" and "necessity" when combined with America's unprecedented military power threatens to nullify the human rights structure and humanitarian legal safeguards constructed by the international community since the end of World War II. In a similar vein, Michael Ignatieff has sharply criticized what he calls "American exceptionalism" on the question of human rights. "American human rights policy in the last twenty years is increasingly distinctive and paradoxical: it is the product of a nation with a great national rights tradition that leads the world in denouncing human rights violations of others but refuses to ratify key international rights conventions itself. The most important resistance to the domestic application of international human rights norms comes not from rogue states outside of the Western tradition or from Islam and Asian societies. It comes, in fact, from within the heart of the Western rights tradition itself, from a nation that, in linking rights to

faulty intelligence, but that fact has not dissuaded the administration from pursuing its military aims as part of its larger "war on terror." The U.S. anti-terror campaign has also resulted in a dramatic constriction of civil liberties as increased surveillance of mail, email messages, and telephone conversations, curtailment of the legal rights of those suspected of terrorist activities, and a dampening of political dissent and criticism have become widespread in the United States in the post–9/11 era.

How ironic, no, how tragic, that we have come to this point just eighteen years since the fall of communist rule in Central and Eastern Europe. You will remember that Francis Fukuyama in his essay and book entitled "The End of History" argued that these democratic revolutions inaugurated the era of "the universalization of Western liberal democracy as the final form of human government."[2] While other commentators were more subtle and careful in their judgments, a widespread consensus arose at that time concerning the triumph of liberal ideas and institutions as a consequence of the failure of communist rule. The fundamental liberal notions concerning the rule of law, the primacy of constitutional legitimacy, the centrality of parliamentary government, and the importance of an independent judiciary filled the vacuum created by the collapse of communist institutions and ideology. Timothy Garton Ash argued that these revolutions offered "no fundamentally new ideas on the big questions of politics, economics, law or international relations. The ideas whose time has come are old, familiar, well-tested ones."[3] Central European political theorists echoed these sentiments. The Polish intellectual Adam Michnik argued that Eastern Europe was faced with the choice of ethnic tribalism on the one hand or liberal democracy on the other. "[L]iberal values in the era of post-communism . . . are meeting with their true renaissance. Through their resistance to communism, they rediscovered their vision of civil liberty, their dreams of parliamentarism, of cultural and political pluralism,

---

popular sovereignty, opposes international human rights oversight as an infringement on its democracy." Michael Ignatieff, *Human Rights as Politics and Idolatry* (Princeton: Princeton University Press, 2001), p. 93.

2. Francis Fukuyama, "The End of History?" *National Interest* 16 (Summer 1989): 3-18. See also *The End of History and the Last Man* (New York: Free Press, 1992), pp. 39-51.

3. Timothy Garton Ash, *The Magic Lantern* (New York: Random House, 1990), p. 154. Ash reiterated this point in his article "Ten Years After," *The New York Review of Books* 46, no. 18 (Nov. 18, 1999): 16-19.

of tolerance, and their desire for a country free of any kind of ideological dictatorship."[4]

My purpose in this essay is not to dispute the judgment that the revolutions in Central and Eastern Europe yielded liberal representative institutions that have brought needed reforms to these countries. Rather, I want to dispute the assertion that the pre-1989 reform movements did not represent democratic values different from those of liberal representative institutions. I believe that movements like Charter 77[5] represented a deeper, more radical form of democratic vision than that inherent within liberal democracies.[6] Moreover, I will argue that such democratic vision remains vital, especially for the churches of Central and Eastern Europe, during this time of the growth and strengthening of their liberal democratic institutions. At this time of international peril we need, more than ever, an authentic witness to a more radical democratic vision, one that springs from the Christian gospel. We need Christian public theologians who serve as "connected critics" within the nascent liberal democratic states of Central Europe.

The values represented by organizations like Charter 77 in the Czech Republic included liberal ideas like individual freedom and constitutional institutions; more importantly, however, those values addressed fundamental issues concerning the nature and function of organizations within civil society. Charter 77 described itself as a "civic initiative," a

---

4. Adam Michnik, "The Presence of Liberal Values," *East European Reporter* 4 (Spring/Summer 1991): 70-72.

5. "Charter 77 was formed in 1976 as an ad hoc community of individuals who sought to protest the arrest of an avant-garde rock band called Plastic People of the Universe. The Charter was formed around the drafting of a declaration of protest that appealed to the principles of legality affirmed by the Helsinki Accords, to which the Czech regime had been a signatory. But it soon became the nucleus of a variety of independent initiatives aimed at the democratization of Czech society." Quoted by Jeffrey C. Isaac, "The Meanings of 1989," in his *Democracy in Dark Times* (Ithaca: Cornell University Press, 1998), p. 161.

6. For an important analysis of these deeper democratic values see, Jeffrey C. Isaac, "The Meanings of 1989"; also cf. Neal Ascherson, "1989 in Eastern Europe: Constitutional Representative Democracy or a 'Return to Normalcy,'" in *Democracy: The Unfinished Journey, 508 BC to AD 1993*, ed. John Dunn (New York: Oxford University Press, 1992). Cf. also Christiane Olivo, *Creating a Democratic Civil Society in Eastern Germany* (New York: PALGRAVE, 2001); Sorin Antohi and Vladimir Tismaneanu, eds., *Between Past and Future: The Revolutions of 1989 and Their Aftermath* (Budapest: Central European University Press, 2000); *The Revolutions of 1989*, ed. Vladimir Tismaneanu (London: Routledge, 1999).

movement within civil society seeking to shape public opinion rather than exercising direct political power. Characterizing its approach as a form of "antipolitical politics,"[7] it sought to "rehabilitate people as the true subjects of history . . . to reach for a new type of politics . . . an effort to revive active citizenship."[8] Václav Havel was especially clear that the Chartist movement critique, while directed primarily at the totalitarian communist regimes, applied to all modern politics, including those of liberal democracy. The targets for Chartist protests were any political system that subjected citizens to "the irrational momentum of impersonal and inhuman power — the power of ideologies, systems, apparat, bureaucracy, artificial languages, and political slogans." This critique included Western-type capitalist liberal democracies in which the individual is treated as "an obedient member of a consumer herd. . . . [I]nstead of a free share in economic decision-making, free participation in political life, and free intellectual advancement, all people are actually offered is a chance freely to choose which washing machine or refrigerator they want to buy."[9] Without the internal critique of more radical democratic civic movements liberal democratic institutions can too easily succumb to the forms of corruption and misuse of power within the reach of any modern political system.

What emerges clearly from the Chartist literature, and from the literature of Central European dissent more generally, is the belief that the impersonality and consumerism of modern society, the bureaucratization of political agencies, and the debasement of political communication through the cynical manipulation of language and images produce a shallow politics, a disengaged citizenry, and the domination of well-organized corporate interests.[10]

7. The term is Vaclav Havel's. See, for example, his "Politics and Conscience," in Václav Havel, *Living in Truth: Twenty-two Essays Published on the Occasion of the Award of the Erasmus Prize to Vaclav Havel*, ed. Jan Vladislav (London & Boston: Faber & Faber, 1987), pp. 136-57.

8. Charter 77, Document no. 2/1985, reprinted in U.S. Congress, Commission on Security and Cooperation in Europe, *Human Rights in Czechoslovakia: The Documents of Charter 77, 1982-1987* (Washington, DC: U.S. Government Printing Office, 1988), pp. 150, 161.

9. Václav Havel, "Dear Dr. Husak," *Open Letters: Selected Writings, 1965-1990* (New York: Vintage, 1992), p. 60.

10. Isaac, "Meanings of 1989," p. 166.

Democratic civic movements often engage in forms of political activity — petition drives, political demonstrations, civil disobedience — designed not to undermine liberal institutions but to call those institutions to a higher ethical standard. These forms of oppositional democratic politics are more rebellious and participatory than the electoral politics characteristic of liberal representative government, and they function primarily as internal critiques within liberal institutions. These movements often embody highly developed ethical perspectives and substantive notions of human dignity and aspirations. In the language of liberal political theory democratic civic movements have a "thick" understanding of "good," one that stands in tension with the "thin" notions necessary to the "overlapping consensus" of pluralist liberal democracies.[11] They operate primarily within the realm of civil society and though their critiques are often addressed to political systems they are dedicated primarily to the creation of more responsible forms of citizenship rather than the direct exercise of political power. These organizations and their leaders function at their best to call modern political societies to a higher standard of behavior, toward more aggressive support for human dignity, to a clearer recognition of their own tendencies toward idolatry and self-aggrandizement. At the same time they call ordinary citizens to a higher degree of democratic participation and a deeper sense of the exercise of civic freedom essential to the healthy operation of modern democratic societies.

It has been understandably difficult for organizations like Charter 77 to keep their oppositional focus in the young democratic republics of which they are a part. The urgent need to build, support, and nurture fragile democratic institutions made criticism seem out of place, even unpatriotic, in the early years following the 1989 revolutions. In addition, the economic and political turmoil of the first post-revolution decade made attention to matters of citizen development seem like a luxury. Finally, the fact that movement leaders such as Havel and Welesa were elected to positions of national leadership reversed their long established roles as governmental critics and forced them to become advocates for liberal democratic institutions.[12] Havel, in particular, continued to speak and write about the

---

11. For an account of these political notions in relation to the question of the role of religion in democratic societies, see Ronald F. Thiemann, *Religion in Public Life: A Dilemma for Democracy* (Georgetown: The Century Fund/Georgetown University Press, 1996), pp. 72-120.

12. "[The] new style of 'forum' or 'civic movement' politics, as opposed to old-style

importance of citizen empowerment, but the demands of being head of state forced him to attend more fully to the mundane problems of everyday governance. As he himself said in the final address of his presidency,

And so — without ever having tried to become a fairy-tale king, and despite finding myself practically forced into this position, through an accident of history as well — I was given no diplomatic immunity from that hard fall to earth, from the exhilarating world of revolutionary excitement into the mundane world of bureaucratic routine. . . . And suddenly I feel that the very same spiritual and intellectual unease that once compelled me to stand up against the totalitarian regime and go to jail for it is now causing me to have such deep doubts about the value of my own work, or the work of those I have supported, or those whose influence I have made possible. . . . There is no more relying on the accidents of history that lift poets into places where empires and military alliances are brought down. The warning voices of poets must be carefully listened to and taken very seriously, perhaps even more seriously than the voices of bankers or stockbrokers. But at the same time, we cannot expect that the world — in the hands of poets — will suddenly be transformed into a poem.[13]

The role of churches and people of faith in the revolutions of 1989 has been widely reported. These revolutions are virtually unimaginable without the essential support, inspiration, and motivation provided by communities of faith. The Catholic Church in Poland and Hungary, the Lutheran churches of East Germany, and the Protestant Hungarian minorities in Ro-

---

Western party politics . . . soon disappeared, to be replaced by local versions of arrangements to be found already somewhere else in the world. These countries now all have conventional, Western-style party politics." Ash, "Ten Years After," p. 18. G. M. Tamas, the Hungarian political philosopher, writes of the unfulfilled hopes of the 1989 revolutions: "Nobody dared to confess that liberal democracy is *not* government by the people, that economic decisions are *not* to be taken by plebiscite. Nobody dared to point out that in liberal democracies there is a conspicuous, loud, assertive political elite (the butt of satirists since Aristophanes), that democratic conformism will be the rule rather than the exception, and that not only are these new elites dazzlingly and deafeningly *obvious,* but also *common.*" G. M. Tamas, "The Legacy of Dissent," in Vladimir Tismaneanu, ed., *The Revolutions of 1989,* p. 195.

13. Václav Havel, "A Farewell to Politics," *The New York Review of Books* 24 (Oct. 24, 2002): 4.

mania all contributed mightily to the fall of the communist regimes. These church communities have an important role in continuing to support the new liberal democratic institutions of their nations. But I want to argue in the concluding portion of this essay that the churches' contributions cannot be limited to their role in underwriting liberal democracy; they must also take on the more prophetic role of becoming "connected critics" within their own societies. The potential corruptibility of liberal regimes, seen so clearly in the current actions of the American government, requires the constant vigilance of communities of faith. No other institution within civil society can possibly play this role with the same integrity and effectiveness as the churches. Organizations like Charter 77 emerge from the necessities of a particular historical moment of crisis and fade away precisely as such crises ease or disappear. The churches, on the other hand, are part of the long-term permanent fabric of civil society and thus provide a potential continuing source of support as well as critique of liberal institutions. But churches can play this complicated role within their nation-states only if they develop a clear and authentic understanding of their status as public theological institutions or communities of connected critics.

I want to set before you an understanding of the public theologian as "connected critic." I have used this notion, which I gratefully borrow from Michael Walzer,[14] in my book *Religion in Public Life: A Dilemma for Democracy*[15] to capture the stance of critique I believe most appropriate for people of faith, disciples who are also citizens, within democratic societies. I now want to expand upon this idea and propose it as a proper understanding of the person of faith as public theologian.

> Hear this word that the LORD has spoken against you, O people of Israel, against the whole family that I brought up out of the land of Egypt: You only have I known of all the families of the earth; therefore I will punish you for all your iniquities. (Amos 3:1-2, NRSV)

> The judgment of God is upon the church as never before. If the church of today does not recapture the sacrificial spirit of the early

---

14. See Michael Walzer, *The Company of Critics: Social Criticism and Political Commitment in the Twentieth Century* (New York: Basic Books, 1988).

15. Ronald F. Thiemann, *Religion in Public Life: A Dilemma for Democracy* (Georgetown: Georgetown University Press/The Century Foundation, 1996).

church, it will lose its authentic ring, forfeit the loyalty of millions, and be dismissed as an irrelevant social club with no meaning. . . . I hope the church as a whole will meet the challenge of this decisive hour. But even if the church does not come to the aid of justice, I have no despair about the future. . . . We will reach the goal of freedom in Birmingham and all over the nation, because the goal of America is freedom. Abused and scorned as we may be, our destiny is tied up with the destiny of America. . . . We will win our freedom because the sacred heritage of our nation and the eternal will of God are embodied in our echoing demands. (Martin Luther King Jr., "Letter from Birmingham City Jail")[16]

The prophet Amos and the prophet Martin capture the essential elements of connected criticism. Amos speaks to the people of Israel as a member of that "whole family . . . brought up out of the land of Egypt." He claims the authority of the God whose very "outstretched arm" had rescued the people from slavery and brought them into the land of promise. It is precisely as a member of the family of Israel, of the common religious and political community, that he speaks the judgment of God to his own people. So, too, Martin Luther King Jr. addresses the white clergy of Birmingham and through them the whole of the church and the whole of the nation as well. He speaks as a fellow churchman and citizen and announces the "judgment of God . . . upon the church." The authority for this word of judgment is the shared though broken covenant expressed in the prophets of Israel, the ministry of Jesus, and the founding documents of the nation. Though he condemns the pernicious segregation of racist America, he finds (or is it creates?) in the biblical and American traditions the sources of both judgment and hope. "We will reach the goal of freedom in Birmingham and all over the nation, because the goal of America is freedom. . . . We will win our freedom because the sacred heritage of our nation and the eternal will of God are embodied in our echoing demands."[17]

Connected criticism of the public theologian oscillates between the poles of critique and connection, solitude and solidarity, alienation and authority. Connected critics are those who are fully engaged in the very

16. James Melvin Washington, ed., *A Testament of Hope: Essential Writings of Martin Luther King, Jr.* (San Francisco: Harper & Row, 1986), pp. 300-301.

17. Washington, ed., *A Testament of Hope*, p. 301.

enterprise they criticize, yet alienated by the deceits and shortcomings of their own community. Because they care so deeply about the values inherent in their common enterprise, they vividly experience the evils of their society even as they call their community back to its better nature. Connected critics recognize that fallibility that clings to the life of every political or social organization, and they seek to identify both the virtuous and the vicious dimensions of the common life in which they participate. Connected critics exemplify both the commitment characteristic of the loyal participant and the critique characteristic of the disillusioned dissenter. This dialectic between commitment and critique is the identifying feature that distinguishes acts of dissent that display genuine moral integrity from those that represent mere expediency or self-interest.

The connected critic is socially situated within the community to which her criticism is directed, yet still finds within the common life of the society principles of justice that serve as the basis for hope. Living in a state of "antagonistic connection" the public theologian through an act of imaginative construction discerns the principles of justice that provide the basis for both critique and hope. Such an imaginative act is simultaneously a matter of discovery and creation. So Abraham Lincoln could *discern* within the founding documents of a nation "half slave and half free" the ideas of freedom and equality penned by the slave-holder Thomas Jefferson and so *create* a new understanding of citizenship within the republic. Likewise Martin Luther King Jr. sitting in his jail cell in Birmingham, Alabama, could *discern*, despite the segregated polity of the South, the freedom which is "the sacred heritage of our nation and the eternal will of God" and so *create* a new "birth of freedom" for African-American citizens.

I believe that this notion of public theologian as connected critic is vital to the future of public theology in Central Europe today. The notion of dual citizenship — being *in* the world but not *of* the world — accurately describes the unique challenges facing the churches of Central Europe as they offer criticisms of their government's actions and policies even as they support the larger project of liberal democratic reform. The churches of Central Europe, like the churches in South Africa, have a unique role and witness to offer to the world today — a vision of public life that offers genuine hope for a more equitable and just society. The emerging democracies of the world have an opportunity to develop conceptions of public life in which constructive criticism and creative opposition are seen to be signs of vitality and health.

By way of conclusion I want to offer an overview of the elements that ought to be included in a vigorous and engaged public theology today.

Democratic vision. Public churches and their theologians cannot simply borrow notions of democracy that have been developed within modern liberal republics. The first task of a Christian public theology is to set forth a vision of freedom, equality, and justice that resonates with the more radical vision of the biblical witness.[18] While this vision may well affirm many of the principles and procedures of modern liberal political theory,[19] it should also hold liberal institutions to a higher standard of freedom and equality. "Let justice roll down like waters and righteousness like a mighty stream" (Amos 5:24). Wherever modern liberal societies erect barriers to genuine equality through discrimination on the basis of race, gender, or sexual orientation a Christian public theology should speak out on the basis of a deeper understanding of equality as those who stand before the God of grace and justice. "There is no longer Jew or Greek, there is no longer slave nor free, there is no longer male and female" (Gal. 3:28). This standard of equality should apply first in the church and then analogously to the public realm. And if we are unable to model such equality in the church itself, then we will surely be of little or no effect in the larger public square. Wherever modern liberal societies accept vast disparities in economic, social, or emotional well-being between their richest and poorest citizens, then Christian public theologians need to speak out in the name and for the sake of those who suffer.[20] "Truly I tell you, just as you did it to one of the least of these who are members of my family, you did it to me" (Matt. 25:40). The most powerful over-arching concept for the democratic vision of Christian public theology is the biblical notion of *Shalom,* the just and gracious reign of God

18. I have addressed these issues in my essay "I Have Heard the Cry of My People: Discerning the Call of God in the Cries of God's People," in Ronald F. Thiemann, *Constructing a Public Theology: The Church in a Pluralistic Culture* (Louisville: Westminster/John Knox, 1991), pp. 96-111. This essay was first developed as the keynote address to the 1990 Lutheran World Federation Assembly in Curitiba, Brazil.

19. These include universal adult suffrage; free and fair elections; proportionate representation; majority decision-making; equality before the law; an independent judiciary; equality of opportunity; freedom to organize politically; freedom of speech, conscience, and dissent; freedom of the press and assembly; the rule of law and "due process"; separation of church and state; and freedom of religion and conscience.

20. See Douglas A. Hicks, *Inequality and Christian Ethics* (Cambridge: Cambridge University Press, 2000).

over all creation.[21] "Thus the wilderness will become garden land and garden land will be reckoned as common as scrub. Justice will make its home in the wilderness, and righteousness dwell in the grassland; righteousness will yield *Shalom*" (Isa. 32:16-17). The cosmos groans in travail awaiting the day of God's *Shalom*, and the churches must once again proclaim and act upon this radical vision of hope and reconciliation.

Social analysis. While democratic vision provides the fundamental basis of a Christian public theology, it cannot simply be applied directly to the realities of modern social and political life. If public theologians are to be effective in addressing the problems facing their democratic societies, they must learn the skills of careful social analysis of the conditions of modernity. Three tendencies of the modern world deserve special attention: the emphasis upon individual autonomy, the exaltation of technical reason and its associated forms of power and control, and fragmentation of community. To the modern emphasis upon individual autonomy, public theology must witness to the sociality of the triune God revealed in Jesus Christ and to solidarity within the human community. To the exaltation of technical reason and its associated forms of power and control, public theology must witness to the theological virtues of faith, hope, and love and their role in creating relationships that eschew manipulation and control of the other. To the fragmentation of community, public theology must witness to the complex vision of unity in plurality that honors both difference and commonality. "Now there are varieties of gifts, but the same Spirit; and there are varieties of services, but the same Lord; and there are varieties of activities, but it is the same God who activates all of them in everyone" (1 Cor. 12:4-6). While witness is the first essential step within public theology, it is not sufficient. The churches must then follow that witness by modeling forms of ministry that exemplify the solidarity of those who worship a triune God, by creating relationships that manifest the theological virtues, and by creating communities in which diversity and commonality embrace one another. The critical social analysis of public theology applies to the churches as well as to the wider societies of which we are a part.

Prophetic critique. On the basis of the democratic vision of *Shalom* and the critical social analysis of church and society, public theology must then proceed to the prophetic critique against the forms of sin, distortion,

---

21. The notion of *Shalom* structures the prophetic vision developed by John W. de Gruchy in *Christianity and Democracy* (Cambridge: Cambridge University Press, 1995).

and oppression that characterize public life within democratic societies. Here the analysis must become local and particular. Churches have often been perceived as irrelevant to their own societies because they have engaged in such broadside moral critiques. Ethical analysis in modern society requires close attention to the details of a specific social situation. General invocations of oppression or denunciation of sin are hardly sufficient for a relevant prophetic critique of modern social conditions. Here we can all learn from the Roman Catholic Church. Both the social statements issued by the U.S. Conference of Catholic Bishops and the papal encyclicals on social issues are characterized by careful theological and social analysis which together yield a form of prophetic critique directed against the specific ills of particular societies. In the United States the evangelical social movement, Call to Renewal, and the reformed Jewish movement, Tikkun, have modeled forms of prophetic critique shaped by careful and detailed analysis of specific political and social situations. It is surely the case that modern liberal societies are beset by some common ills: the accumulation of power, both economic and political, in the hands of elites; the alienation of individual citizens from the political process; the progressive privatization of civil society and the loss of engaged citizenship; the increasing distance between policy makers/policy experts and ordinary citizens; the continuing degradation of the environment; the reemergence of forms of xenophobia, racism, and discrimination. Still, for prophetic critique to be effective, the word of justice must be applied to an analysis of the particular forms of injustice present in a specific society.

    Acts of resistance/emancipation. The bureaucratic structure of churches in the West has made it difficult for church bodies to engage in significant acts of resistance and/or emancipation in their own societies. By and large the major Protestant churches have used the "social statement" as the primary form of address to issues in public life. These statements, written by church bureaucrats and passed at church assemblies, have little effect either on the laity of the church or upon political leaders. As we have learned from organizations like Charter 77, genuine engagement of public life by organizations in civil society requires involvement in participatory forms of oppositional democracy. Genuine acts of resistance involve people gathering together at rallies, in protest demonstrations, and in ways in which bodies actually fill public space. It is difficult to motivate people of privilege to engage in these more radical bodily forms of protest, in large part because they (we?) benefit enormously from the very liberal institutions we might be called upon to critique. In the US the Industrial Areas Foundation has focussed most of its organizational efforts around religious communities.[22] The IAF "network engages faith traditions in an effort to construct a politics that addresses the concrete needs of families in low-income communities of color and working Americans more broadly. . . . [T]he deep religious faith of people and the support they receive from fellow parishioners help generate the vision and confidence necessary to enter the public arena as leaders of long-neglected communities."[23] IAF organizations like the Greater Boston Interfaith Organization have had significant success in linking inner-city and suburban churches in alliances for affordable housing in the Boston area. While the inner-city parishes set the agenda for IAF organizing, suburban churches add financial support and political clout at appropriate moments in the process. As the churches of Central Europe seek to find appropriate forms by which prophetic critique can yield effective acts of resistance, these faith-based organizing efforts might be helpful models to examine. By contrast the highly bureaucratized organizations of the so-called "mainline" churches offer little to study or emulate.

Acts of reconciliation. The Jewish and Christian vision of *Shalom* for the entire creation of God offers the hope that genuine peace can be accomplished through the action of a just and gracious God. This vision also recognizes that human sin and corruption make it necessary to engage in prophetic critique and acts of resistance and emancipation. At the same time, the vision of *Shalom* inspires us to risk acts of reconciliation whenever the opportunity for genuine peacemaking arises. One of the remarkable qualities of Martin Luther King Jr. was his ability to see beyond the limitations of the present-day struggle to that horizon of hope and reconciliation at the journey's end. In his remarkable "Letter from Birmingham City Jail" Dr. King engaged in just the kind of public theological reflection I have outlined in this essay. In the midst of his prophetic critique and his efforts to organize acts of resistance he never lost sight of a future that his faith-filled democratic vision set before his eyes. "Let us hope that the dark clouds of racial prejudice will soon pass away and the deep fog of misunderstanding will be lifted from our fear-drenched communities and in

22. See Mark R. Warren, *Dry Bones Rattling: Community Building to Revitalize American Democracy* (Princeton: Princeton University Press, 2001).

23. Warren, *Dry Bones Rattling,* pp. 4-5.

some not too distant tomorrow the radiant stars of love and brotherhood will shine over our great nation with all of their scintillating beauty."[24] In like manner the Truth and Reconciliation process in South Africa directly engaged the acts of terror, torture, and oppression of the apartheid regime and then sought the means whereby genuine justice and reconciliation could be restored to that racially torn nation. Timothy Garton Ash has recently argued that the peaceful revolutions of Central Europe, for all of their remarkable accomplishments, have

> missed a sense of revolutionary catharsis. . . . The result has been a widespread sense of frustration. If you travel through Central Europe today, you will be told again and again by ordinary men and women that "the same people are still on top," that the communists have become the worst capitalists, that "more should have been done" to make a reckoning with the past. . . . I believe . . . that all the countries of Central Europe could and should have tried the expedient of a truth commission . . . before which the political leaders of the former regime and those accused of crime under it have to testify. . . . It symbolically draws a line between the new era and the old, without calling for forgetting or even, necessarily, forgiving. It is probably the closest a nonrevolutionary can come to revolutionary catharsis.[25]

I leave it to colleagues in the churches of Central Europe to determine whether Ash's suggestion has merit. But if some more public act of confession and reconciliation is still called for, surely the churches should play a crucial role in shaping this important public ritual.[26]

---

24. Martin Luther King Jr., "Letter from Birmingham City Jail," in Washington, *A Testament of Hope*, p. 301.

25. Ash, "Ten Years After," p. 18.

26. The Evangelical Church of Slovakia is currently struggling with the aftermath of the opening of the secret police files. In a conference, "The Church in the Struggle with the Totalitarian Regime — Yesterday and Today," held recently at the Bible College in Martin, Slovakia, church leaders spoke openly about the need to come to terms with the past, especially the collaboration of many church leaders with the Communist regime. The conference was sparked by revelations that Catholic Archbishop Jan Sokol and Lutheran bishop Julius Filo are both identified in the files as agents of the secret police. Both leaders have vigorously denied the charges, but the debate within the churches and nations continues.

This outline of the principles of public theology as connected criticism can only hint at the directions in which public theology might develop within Central Europe today. For those of us in the West, and particularly for Americans like myself, our deep disappointment and frustration with our own government lead us to look to places like Southern Africa and Central Europe for new and more hopeful forms of engagement between communities of faith and their own liberal democratic governments. If the churches in these regions can engage in courageous yet humble acts of discipleship and public leadership, then they can serve as a beacon of hope for all who struggle to live lives of faithfulness and integrity during this time of peril. For finally we shall be judged not by our theologies but by our faithfulness to a crucified and risen Lord who bids us "come and follow."

Persuasion and Indoctrination in Lutheran Colleges

Gerald R. McDermott

The thinker without a paradox is like a lover without feeling: a paltry mediocrity.

Søren Kierkegaard, *Philosophical Fragments*

Religious truth is not only a portion but a condition of general knowledge.

John Henry Newman, *The Idea of the University*

The slenderest acquaintance we can form with heavenly things is more desirable than a thorough grasp of mundane matters.

Thomas Aquinas, *Summa Theologiae*
(quoting Aristotle, *De partibus animalium*)

There is no work more worthy of pope or emperor than a thorough reform of the universities. . . . I would advise no one to send his child where the Holy Scriptures are not supreme. Every institution that does not unceasingly pursue the study of God's word becomes corrupt.

Martin Luther, "To the Christian Nobility of the German Nation Concerning the Reform of the Christian Estate"

Many in the academy think it illegitimate for the college professor to seek to persuade students of moral or philosophical propositions. They reason that it is the responsibility of the professor to present all subject matter from a position of philosophical neutrality, and that to do otherwise is both a compromise of the teacher's integrity and the student's right not to be indoctrinated. Hence for a professor to seek to persuade students of a moral, philosophical, or religious proposition is a flight from the Enlightenment ideal of objectivity to the medieval tyranny of dogmatism and indoctrination.

It is because of this line of thinking (as well as some others) that some scholar/teachers in Lutheran colleges question efforts to introduce students to Christian approaches to reality and learning. They argue that the presentation of any subject in the classroom that presupposes the normative value of Christian perspectives so distorts the subject that learning is necessarily diminished if not subverted.

The result, oddly enough, is church-related education that marginalizes what the church prizes. Professors either trivialize or deny the significance of faith in learning at colleges whose founders were convinced of the integral connection between faith and learning. All too often teachers at Lutheran colleges think it anathema to promote faith in the classroom, or even to discuss openly the impact of faith on their discipline. They think it their duty to treat their subject matter and especially religion with detached objectivity, which for many means neutrality. To profess faith in the classroom, they believe, would be unprofessional.

In this essay I first show how the Lutheran academy got to be this way — by uncritically adopting narrow views of reason and knowledge from certain Enlightenment traditions[1] and then using this constricted vision to read Luther and Bonhoeffer in odd ways. In the second section I challenge Enlightenment presumptions about fact and opinion, neutrality, and intellectual autonomy. Finally, at the end of the essay, I propose a new model for pedagogy in the Lutheran college classroom, one that can speak of faith without indoctrination.

---

1. Of course in this respect Lutherans were not distinctive, but followed the general trends of Western thinking.

How Did We Get Here?

Therefore, before I argue that this disconnect between faith and learning — and its consequent rejection of persuasion — are untenable, I will explore how we got here. That is, how did church-related colleges move in less than a century from schools that sought to present all of life and learning from a faith perspective to institutions that regard theology as inimical to what is taught in most classrooms?

In this section I propose that three lines of thinking led to our current situation. First, Western thinkers came to confuse persuasion with indoctrination; second, these same thinkers adopted narrowly constricted understandings of reason and knowledge; and third, certain Lutheran thinkers misunderstood Luther's doctrine of the Two Kingdoms.

First, many Lutheran academics distrust persuasion because it seems to smack of indoctrination. This has come from the Enlightenment's preference for the "philosophical" over the "oratorical" ideal of the liberal arts. As Elmer John Thiessen has shown, the liberal arts are rooted in these two ancient Greek intellectual ideals. The first emphasized the never-ending search for truth, epitomized by Socrates as freethinker, critic, and social gadfly. The Enlightenment particularly seized upon this Greek ideal to redefine "liberal" to mean free from prejudice and open-minded.

The second Greek ideal was the oratorical. This stressed the need to pass traditions on to the uninitiated, and assumed that Socrates and others found notions that were finally true. Its aim was to teach virtues already known rather than to continue searching.

While these ideals coexisted in a kind of symbiotic tension during the medieval and early modern periods, Enlightenment thinkers gave new life to the Greek philosophical ideal because of the carnage they suffered in the wake of the seventeenth-century wars of religion. Appeals to religious authority and tradition, which emphasized differences rather than similarities among religions, seemed responsible for the conflicts and resulting social devastation. Hence Enlightenment thinkers became determined to rely on evidences from nature and reason that seemed universally accessible. They viewed the particular and historical with suspicion, and thought of learning as based on freedom (from authority), autonomy, individualism, equality, toleration, critical rationality, science, and belief in progress.

Kant particularly imprinted the idea of autonomy on the modern consciousness. The ideal society was thought to be composed of individuals who voluntarily submit to a moral law arising from within. The aim of liberal education was to get people to think for themselves rather than submit to indoctrination, which was thought to discourage curiosity and criticism.

The twentieth-century rise of fascism and communism reinforced fears of indoctrination. Teaching normative truths came to be considered authoritarian, intolerant, bigoted (because it teaches exclusive claims to truth), and threatening to individual rights because of its appeals to a community's beliefs. Persuasion then became associated with superstition and false consciousness, in contrast to "progressive," "open," and "scientific" teaching.[2]

Second, the relatively recent constriction in understandings of "reason" and "knowledge" has also contributed to the disfavor with which persuasion (to moral and metaphysical principles) has come to be viewed. One of the hallmarks of modernity has been what Douglas Sloan calls a "two-realm theory of truth." Real knowledge is typically thought to come only through science and discursive or empirical reason, while the provenance of meaning and morals is restricted to feeling, tradition, or ineffable experience. Hence the modern world has drawn a sharp distinction between each of the two terms in the following pairs: subject and object, fact and value, the scientific and the human, faith and knowledge. This narrow definition of knowledge has been applied to every level of reality: only what can be measured and quantified, and validated by the scientific method, counts as real knowledge. The deliverances of ethics, religion, and philosophy may be comforting or provocative, but unless derived from quantifiable data are little more than hopeful speculation or arbitrary moralizing.[3]

Sloan argues that America's most prominent religious thinkers in the twentieth century accepted this two-realm theory of truth rather uncritically. Paul Tillich, Reinhold Niebuhr, and H. Richard Niebuhr recognized nineteenth-century positivism's arbitrary restriction of knowledge to the narrow realm of sensory phenomena, and labored mightily to make room for ontological and ecstatic reason (Tillich), practical knowledge and the knowledge of persons (Reinhold Niebuhr), and inner and outer history and the role of the imagination in knowledge (H. Richard Niebuhr). They

2. Elmer John Thiessen, *Teaching for Commitment: Liberal Education, Indoctrination, and Christian Nurture* (Montreal and Kingston: McGill-Queen's University Press, 1994), pp. 34-47.

3. Douglas Sloan, *Faith and Knowledge: Mainline Protestantism and American Higher Education* (Louisville: Westminster, 1994), pp. ix, 114-44.

also began to open up thinking about qualitative knowledge in the knowing of persons, and insisted that metaphor and symbol are the ways to knowing the invisible and metaphysical realms.[4]

At the same time, however, they also insisted that symbols are never to be interpreted literally, and that there is no identification of the sign in the symbol with the referent to which it points. Thus, for fear of objectifying and manipulating objects of religious knowing, Tillich and the Niebuhrs "pulled back from affirming unambiguously the real possibility of knowledge of God and the spiritual world." Yet they affirmed the value of objective, analytic modes of knowing from science and history for every other domain besides faith. Technical reason was the *only* mode of approach to the sensible world. Religious symbol could provide a *sense* of the mystery of existence, but no real knowledge of qualities of everyday reality. Hence they left the structures of reality given by technical, analytical reason "completely unaltered." Therefore the realms of real meaning and ordinary reality were two different worlds, with no integral connection between the two.[5]

Sloan concludes that for all their emphasis on personal and symbolic knowledge, the role of symbols for Tillich and the Niebuhrs is vague. They serve more "for eliciting moods, feelings, energies and existential commitments than for conveying qualitative realities having cognitive significance." But they accept without question a scientific description of nature as a world of impersonal objects related exclusively by physical cause and effect.[6]

Symbols could not be anything but vague, Sloan suggests, because these thinkers swallowed without blinking the Kantian proposition that the *ding-an-sich* can never be known. They recall Kant's famous, "I have found it necessary to deny knowledge of God, freedom and immortality in order to find a place for faith." But that has not been the only problem. They and others have adopted uncritically a host of modernist assumptions: the notion that the world is made up of inanimate and insentient matter related solely by determinate and mechanical cause and effect; the idea that all our knowledge must be rooted in or related to sense experience; the dogma that consciousness arises from what is insentient and un-

4. Sloan, *Faith and Knowledge*, pp. 115-18.
5. Sloan, *Faith and Knowledge*, pp. 120, 121.
6. Sloan, *Faith and Knowledge*, pp. 122, 125.

conscious; the assumption that mind is nothing more than a product of chemical brain processes; the presupposition that all statements about quality — meaning, values, ideals, spirit — can be reduced to some more fundamental quantitative substrata, or are merely subjective expressions of arbitrary preferences, personal or collective; the presumption that genuine knowing comes through the "objective onlooker."[7]

Sloan points out that while these are assumptions of modernity, postmoderns cling to all of them except the last, and then run the rest to their extremes. None of the forementioned thinkers — and precious few postmoderns for that matter — seriously consider alternatives, such as the possibility of real knowledge of non-sensory and supersensible realities. Sloan complains that little effort is made to develop the suggestions made by Michael Polanyi that all knowledge contains mystery and uncertainty, and that therefore in our knowing we must entrust ourselves to the "intimations of the unseen." Nor do many epistemologists explore Coleridge's insistence on the intuitive dimension in all knowing, or the proposal made by both Samuel Coleridge and Rudolf Steiner that qualities are both objective and subjective.[8]

A third factor contributing to the denigration of persuasion in the Lutheran academy has been an interpretation of Luther's Two Kingdoms doctrine that suggests a radical dissociation of faith from reason. By two kingdoms,[9] Luther meant two ways in which God rules the world. God's right hand is the gospel, through which he rules in person, through his ministers, the Word and sacraments. In the "orders of creation" (state, economy, family, and even church) human beings encounter God's left hand, the law, through which God rules but veiled behind a mask. According to Luther, God's ultimate aim is the same for each — victory over evil and the reconciliation of the world to himself — but the two kinds of rule represent different strategies to reach that end. One seeks justice and order in this life, the other salvation, both in this life and beyond.[10] As George

7. Sloan, *Faith and Knowledge*, pp. 127, 212-19.

8. Sloan, *Faith and Knowledge*, pp. 218, 198, 219, 234-37.

9. Actually Karl Barth was the first to apply this term to what had been more generally known as "God's twofold rule." Robert Benne, *The Paradoxical Vision: A Public Theology for the Twenty-first Century* (Minneapolis: Fortress, 1995), pp. 78-79.

10. See Martin Luther, "Temporal Authority: To What Extent It Should Be Obeyed," in *Martin Luther's Basic Theological Writings*, ed. Timothy Lull (Minneapolis: Fortress Press, 1989), pp. 655-703; George W. Forell, *Faith Active in Love: An Investigation of the Principles*

Forell has put it, the secular realm represented by the orders of creation is secular but "not at all secular in the modern sense of the word." There is no realm in all of creation that is independent of God or ultimately removed from his realm.[11]

Yet modern Protestant interpreters of this doctrine have tended to render this doctrine as Luther's attempt to "set the world free for autonomous secularity."[12] When applied to higher education, the most pointed interpretations have taken Luther to be saying that reason is to be left unfettered by the constraints of dogmatic faith; the university is administered through God's left hand, which points the way through unconstrained reason. To submit reason to faith, it is said, is to suppress a gift of creation in the name of dialogue between faith and reason; indeed it violates academic freedom. Reason is free to be God's gift only when it is dissociated from faith, particularly when it rests on self-evident dictates of the rational process or makes inferences from the data of sensory experience. If reason then conflicts with faith, so much the worse for faith, which must be shaped by analytical and empirical reason.[13]

Underlying Luther's Social Ethics (Minneapolis: Augsburg, 1954), pp. 112-55; Benne, *The Paradoxical Vision*, pp. 78-96; John R. Stephenson, "The Two Governments and the Two Kingdoms in Luther's Thought," *Scottish Journal of Theology* 34 (1981): 321-37.

11. Forell, *Faith Active in Love*, p. 131.

12. David S. Yeago, "On Worldly Government: Martin Luther's Political Theology Revisited," unpublished paper, p. 22. For examples of this approach, Benne cites an unnamed Lutheran jurist who said that issues of public life "should remain untouched by the proclamation of the gospel, completely untouched." He also quotes nineteenth-century Lutheran theologian Christian Luthardt: "The gospel has absolutely nothing to do with outward existence but only with eternal life. . . . It is not the vocation of Jesus Christ or of the gospel to change the orders of secular life and establish them anew. . . . Christianity wants to change the person's heart, not his external situation." Benne, *The Paradoxical Vision*, p. 79. This is intriguingly similar to doctrines of the "spirituality of the church" used by antebellum preachers in the American South to ward off Northern challenges to slavery. See, for example, James Henley Thornwell, "A Southern Address to Christendom," in *American Christianity: An Historical Interpretation with Representative Documents*, 2 vols., ed. H. Shelton Smith et al. (New York: Charles Scribner's Sons, 1963), vol. 1, pp. 205-10.

13. See, for example, Mark U. Edwards Jr., "Christian Colleges: A Dying Light or a New Refraction?" *Christian Century*, 21-28 April 1999, 461: "There should be in most cases no substantive difference between scholarship by Christians and by non-Christians. . . . Christian substance appears in the Christian calling of faculty, staff and students and in the Christian context surrounding the academic enterprise — only rarely in the results of scholarly inquiry itself." Benne observes, "Instead of providing room for a dialogue between the gos-

These interpretations have sometimes appealed for support to cryptic notes at the end of Dietrich Bonhoeffer's *Letters and Papers from Prison*. In this short passage (less than two pages) Bonhoeffer remarked that it was time for a kind of secularity in which Christians live as if God were not there. His generation, he wrote, was experiencing a "coming of age" in which God was teaching that "we must live as men who can get along very well without him." They were to live "without using [God] as a working hypothesis."

After appearing to legitimate what became the "death of God" theology of the 1960s, Bonhoeffer explained in the next few sentences what he meant: God on the cross shows us that he conquers not by power but through weakness, in irony and paradox.

> God allows himself to be edged out of the world and on to the cross. God is weak and powerless in the world, and that is exactly the way, the only way in which he can be with us and help us. Matthew 8.17 makes it crystal clear that it is not by his omnipotence that Christ helps us, but by his weakness and suffering. . . . Man's religiosity makes him look in his distress to the power of God in the world; he uses God as a *Deus ex machina*. The Bible however directs him to the powerlessness and suffering of God; only a suffering God can help. To this extent we may say that the process we have described by which the world came of age was an abandonment of a false conception of God, and a clearing of the decks for the God of the Bible, who conquers power and space in the world by his weakness. This must be the starting point for our "worldly" interpretation.[14]

---

pel (in its full trinitarian account of reality) and the law (the realm of secular learning), this faulty interpretation of the Lutheran teaching on the two ways that God reigns (law and gospel) robs the Christian account of any epistemological status. It does this by narrowly defining the gospel as the doctrine of justification, which is preached in the chapel and taught by the theology department. But the gospel is not the full-blown Christian account of reality explicit in the trinitarian faith. It does not have the intellectual content of the Christian account. Therefore, the gospel, in this fuller sense, cannot engage secular learning. In effect, the two ways of knowing — the Christian account given by revelation and the many accounts offered by secular reason — are kept apart." Robert Benne, *Quality with Soul: How Six Premier Colleges Keep Faith with Their Religious Traditions* (Grand Rapids: Eerdmans, 2001), pp. 43-44.

14. Dietrich Bonhoeffer, *Letters and Papers from Prison* (New York: Macmillan, 1953), pp. 219-20.

Several things are clear from this selection. First, Bonhoeffer is referring not to the death of God per se but the death of an old, unbiblical view of God. This is not secularism, where consideration of God is removed from the public realms of government and education, but the elimination of a theology of glory to make room for a theology of the cross. Second, by the world "coming of age" Bonhoeffer means a world that now realizes that the true God does not rescue by power but works mysteriously through defeat and suffering. Third, the world is not to be autonomous in a life free from God but free from a false, pagan view of God in which the deity is a "god of the gaps" who occasionally intervenes to grease an otherwise well-oiled machine.

In his earlier treatise on ethics, Bonhoeffer had denounced the "secularist autonomy" interpretation of Luther's Two Kingdoms doctrine. This was a "pseudo-Lutheran scheme" that was "in profound contradiction to the thought of the Bible and to the thought of the Reformation." The "two spheres" do not exist "in themselves" or "on their own account" but "have their reality nowhere save in the reality of God, in Christ."[15] Bonhoeffer believed Luther developed the doctrine as a way to create theological grounding for his use of the state to help him reform the Roman church.

> Luther was protesting against a Christianity which was striving for independence and detaching itself from the reality in Christ. [By this Bonhoeffer probably meant Luther's proclamation of the independence of the state from clerical control in the name of a medieval Catholicism that asserted papal supremacy over secular rulers.] He protested with the help of the secular and in the name of a better Christianity. . . . It is only in this sense, as a polemical unity, that Luther's doctrine of the two kingdoms is to be accepted, and it was no doubt in this sense that it was originally intended.[16]

It appears, then, that Luther's doctrine of the Two Kingdoms cannot be used to support a radical autonomy for reason, dissociated from truth claims made by faith. In the next section I will argue that recent developments in the philosophy of science and other disciplines show that reason and faith are in fact interdependent.

15. Bonhoeffer, *Ethics*, ed. Eberhard Bethge (New York: Macmillan, 1955), pp. 196-98.
16. Bonhoeffer, *Ethics*, p. 199.

Problems with the Enlightenment Model of Faith and Learning

Now that we have seen some of the factors that contributed to a widespread dissociation of faith from reason, and its concomitant suspicion of persuasion toward moral or theological propositions, it is time to ask whether these attitudes can be sustained. That is, we must ascertain the validity of the "progressive" Enlightenment ideal of teaching and learning, which regards the humanities, particularly philosophy and religion, as matters of "opinion" prone to indoctrination and therefore inimical to persuasion. This Enlightenment approach sees the "secular" disciplines, especially the sciences, as objective presentations of "facts."

A recent generation of scholars in many disciplines thinks this view naive. Take science, for example, the supposed paragon of objectivity. As Thiessen relates the story, since the seventeenth century we have been told that science is based on empiricality, objectivity, and rationality. Empirical data impress themselves upon the observer through the senses (empiricality), the observer collects the data without preconceptions or theories (objectivity), and then concludes in rigorously logical fashion (rationality).[17]

But philosophers of science since Thomas Kuhn have rejected this theory of "immaculate perception."[18] They have portrayed the scientific method in practice as full of imaginative leaps. Einstein confessed, "There is no logical path leading to [discovery] of highly universal laws. They are only to be reached by intuition based upon something like an intellectual love. . . . The mechanics of discovery are neither logical nor intellectual. It's a sudden illumination, almost a rapture. . . . [I]nitially there is a great leap of the imagination."[19]

Little wonder that the philosopher Quine said there is little difference between the theoretical entities posited by science and the gods posited by religion.[20] As Thiessen puts it, both disciplines are human enterprises, shot through with elements of subjectivity but not entirely subjective, and both searching for truth. Both use a variety of criteria including but not limited to empirical data: coherence, simplicity, elegance, explanatory power. If

17. Thiessen, *Teaching for Commitment*, p. 81.
18. Thiessen, *Teaching for Commitment*, p. 81.
19. Albert Einstein, quoted by Lesslie Newbigin, *The Gospel in a Pluralist Society* (Grand Rapids: Eerdmans, 1989), p. 31.
20. W. W. Quine, *From a Logical Point of View* (Cambridge, MA: Harvard University Press, 1961), pp. 20-46; quoted in Thiessen, *Teaching for Commitment*, p. 84.

Kuhn is right, scientists are just as capable of being blinded by their preconceptions as anyone else.[21]

Indoctrination? Philosopher of science Paul Feyerabend argues that scientific "facts" are taught in schools in the same manner in which religious "facts" were taught a century ago. "At the universities the situation is even worse, for indoctrination is here carried out in a much more systematic manner."[22] Malcolm Muggeridge goes even further: "The dogmatism of science has become a new orthodoxy, disseminated by the Media and a State educational system with a thoroughness and subtlety far exceeding anything of the kind achieved by the Inquisition."[23] Feyerabend and Muggeridge are not referring to established scientific inferences based on empirical data, such as gravity and entropy, but methodological scientism that makes religious proclamations about the origin and meaning of the cosmos.[24]

Three charges are typically made to support the notion that persuasion is indoctrination when it concerns religious or philosophical matters. The first is that this is merely the teaching of doctrine, which means inculcating notions without providing sufficient evidence and reasons for proving those notions beyond any doubt.

21. Thiessen, *Teaching for Commitment*, p. 84.

22. Paul Feyerabend, "How to Defend Society against Science," in E. D. Klemke, R. Hollinger, et al., *Introductory Readings in the Philosophy of Science* (Buffalo, NY: Prometheus, 1988), p. 36; quoted in Thiessen, *Teaching for Commitment*, p. 80.

23. Malcolm Muggeridge, *Jesus: The Man Who Lives* (London: Fontana/Collins, 1975), p. 25; quoted in Thiessen, *Teaching for Commitment*, pp. 74-75.

24. Examples of the latter abound. There is, for example, the opening verse to Carl Sagan's TV series, "Cosmos": "The cosmos is all there is, was, or ever will be." One thinks, too, of Richard Dawkins's statement that "the more you understand the significance of evolution, the more you are pushed away from the agnostic position and towards atheism." Dawkins, "A Scientist's Case Against God," *The Independent*, 20 April 1992. Or Stephen Jay Gould's pronouncement, "No intervening spirit watches lovingly over the affairs of nature (though Newton's clock-winding god might have set up the machinery at the beginning of time and then let it run). No vital forces propel evolutionary change. And whatever we think of God, his existence is not manifest in the products of nature." Stephen Jay Gould, "In Praise of Charles Darwin," in *Darwin's Legacy*, ed. Charles L. Hamrum (San Francisco: Harper and Row, 1983), pp. 6-7. Or the "Statement on Teaching Evolution" passed by the National Association of Biology Teachers in 1998 that evolution is "an unsupervised, impersonal, and unpredictable and natural process of temporal descent from genetic modification that is affected by natural selection, chance, historical contingencies, and changing environments." The statement was withdrawn later only after protests from Alvin Plantinga and Huston Smith. Richard John Neuhaus, "The Public Square," *First Things* 80 (February 1998): 75.

The problem with this criterion is that no discipline of learning passes muster, least of all science. Michael Polanyi has shown that the scientific enterprise depends on a community of scientists governed by tradition and authority. Scientists do not learn by proving beyond a doubt every step in every process of the innumerable processes which are held to be so. Instead there is an apprenticeship of pupils to masters, "a modern version of the Apostolic Succession."[25] A master can teach an apprentice only if the apprentice can follow the master's example and assimilate unconsciously rules of which neither may be explicitly aware. Hence an apprentice is one who surrenders herself to some extent uncritically to the imitation of another. While she is learning, the apprentice must accept the master's judgments even when she does not know the evidence for them. As Wittgenstein put it, "The child learns by believing the adult. Doubt comes after belief."[26]

As the eminent education philosopher R. S. Peters recognized, all teaching — in fact all communication — is to some degree concerned with conveying correct beliefs (doctrines, if you will).[27] And all teaching fails to some extent to provide reasons for what is taught. We are finite and so are our students. By the nature of the case we are not able to give sufficient reasons for all our statements and conclusions, much less for the presuppositions upon which our disciplines rest.

So we are all dogmatists to some degree. William James's statement was exaggerated but not wholly amiss: "The greatest empiricists among us are only empiricists on reflection: when left to their instincts, they dogmatize like infallible popes."[28]

Hence if indoctrination means teaching things for which there is not sufficient evidence to dispel *all* doubt, then all scientific theorizing is guilty. According to Feyerabend, no scientific theory ever fits all the rele-

---

25. Michael Polanyi, *Science, Faith and Society* (Chicago and London: University of Chicago Press, 1964), p. 44; quoted in Thiessen, *Teaching for Commitment*, p. 82.

26. Ludwig Wittgenstein, *On Certainty,* ed. G. E. M. Anscombe and G. H. von Wright (New York: Harper and Row, 1972), para. 1; quoted by Thiessen, *Teaching for Commitment,* p. 162. The paragraph on apprenticeship is based on Thiessen, *Teaching for Commitment,* p. 115.

27. R. S. Peters, *Education and the Education of Teachers* (Boston: Routledge, 1977); quoted in Thiessen, *Teaching for Commitment,* p. 102.

28. William James, *Essays in Pragmatism* (New York: Haffner, 1968), p. 67; quoted in Thiessen, *Teaching for Commitment,* p. 103.

vant observations. There are scientific judgments, such as those concerning gravity and entropy mentioned earlier, that are beyond reasonable doubt. But none are beyond *all* doubt. So when scientists accept a theory, they do so without *absolute* clarity of evidence.[29] My point is not that we should suspect the validity of the scientific enterprise, but that while all good theorizing is based on careful groundwork, none — either in the humanities or the sciences — is beyond all doubt.

A second charge made against persuasion in religious and philosophical matters is that the attempt to persuade necessarily hinders the student's growth toward intellectual autonomy. Thiessen argues that what is often presupposed in this charge is an absolute ideal of autonomy that is unrealistic — something like Sartre's self-defining person constructing a self out of nothingness.

Human being, however, is essentially relational and embedded in concrete particularity. We are never as independent as we like to think. One could even say that to suppose that we are or can be autonomous is the primal sin and fundamental illusion.

Besides, the best critical reflection occurs within a community of shared convictions. Individuals in these communities can achieve a measure of autonomy, but they can never wholly distance themselves from their traditions — and this includes the tradition that suspects all tradition. Marxists or feminists can liberate themselves from received traditions but their thinking and willing are always conditioned by their Marxist and feminist traditions.

All autonomy involves some submission. The grad student must submit her preconceptions and preferences to her advisor, the vice-president to the president, and the husband to his wife (if he wants to stay married with a modicum of happiness!). Real(istic) autonomy involves only procedural independence. The Marxist decides freely to submit to a Marxist way of being in the world. The feminist chooses without coercion to submit to a feminist way of seeing and doing. They combine procedural autonomy with substantive dependence. Like the nun who freely chooses to submit to her order's discipline. Substantive dependence with procedural autonomy.[30]

---

29. Paul Feyerabend, *Against Method: Outline of an Anarchistic Theory of Knowledge* (London: Vreson Edition/NLB, 1975); cited in Thiessen, *Teaching for Commitment*, p. 69.

30. The idea of substantive dependence with procedural autonomy is from Thiessen, *Teaching for Commitment*, pp. 130-39.

Thiessen proposes that Christian discipleship works similarly. Disciples freely choose to follow Christ; they don't submit out of mere traditionalism (Mark 7:6-13). The Scriptures condemn passive obedience (Isa. 41:21; Rom. 12:1-2; 1 John 4:1) and encourage critical reflection (James 1:22-25; 1 Cor. 11:27-32).[31] Substantive dependence but procedural autonomy.

Therefore teachers can seek to persuade and promote autonomy at the same time. Christian teachers can do both because they commend a faith that accepts autonomy as a value — a faith that opens itself to future revision or even rejection.

According to Thiessen, the exercise of autonomy and the nurture of autonomy are not the same tasks. It is impossible to nurture a student into critical reflection and openness by themselves. Criticism presupposes content to be criticized. Only if a student has been introduced to a tradition will she have the resources to develop critical faculties.[32]

Thiessen proffers research in developmental psychiatry and psychology by Urie Bronfenbrenner and Michael Rutter to show that exposing a young child to a variety of belief systems too soon will prevent development of abilities necessary for later autonomy. Jean Piaget demonstrated that children must pass through the stages of authority-oriented learning before they could think more autonomously, and that no matter what the age, stages could not be skipped.[33]

Young adults show a similar intellectual development. The goal of the liberal arts is a measure of autonomy, but the nurture needed to achieve that goal will involve differing degrees of autonomy along the way. Christian teachers can know that while they introduce students to a tradition of faith that requires submission to a way of seeing and doing, tradition at the same time liberates its subjects from dependence on other ways of seeing and doing. There is a new autonomy (salvation) that comes from a new vision.

This new vision is also enabling and empowering. As Bruce Reichenbach argues, "profession" based on reasons not compulsion or *mere* authority (this kind of "profession" is roughly equivalent to what I call persuasion) enables students to become — forgive me for using this overworked mantra — critical thinkers. It provides "the intellectual tools to be able to distinguish true from false claims, good from bad reasoning, fact from wishful

31. Thiessen, *Teaching for Commitment*, pp. 135, 139.
32. Thiessen, *Teaching for Commitment*, p. 142.
33. Thiessen, *Teaching for Commitment*, p. 142.

thinking, evidence from pseudoevidence or emotional appeal." Persuasion that is grounded in clear thinking empowers students so that they can more clearly evaluate other claims (especially their professors') that come their way. They are then "enabled to come to an open-minded, fair, reasoned, judicious, and carefully qualified position of their own."[34]

A third challenge to persuasion in religious and philosophical matters is that such persuasion represents close-mindedness. Only by being neutral in such matters can one be truly open-minded. But the fact that one is promoting normative truth means that one cannot be open to alternative ways of thinking. Such openness precludes belief in any kind of absolute truth.

This challenge presumes that it is possible to be open to any and every alternative, and that some of us are that open. But are we? Thiessen marshals an impressive array of contemporary thinkers to suggest that we are not. From Peter Berger's *Sacred Canopy* he argues that we all use "plausibility structures" to reinforce beliefs we hold. Of necessity, then, we all are closed toward views we reject, and are probably less critical toward our own beliefs than we think we are. To be absolutely open to every alternative would mean confronting cognitive dissonance on a massive and regular scale — a prospect we cannot tolerate for very long.[35]

Thiessen cites Polanyi's contention that all our knowing has a tacit dimension — knowledge we are not conscious of and hence unable to specify.

34. Bruce R. Reichenbach, "On Being a Professor: The Case of Socrates," in *Should God Get Tenure? Essays on Religion and Higher Education*, ed. David W. Gill (Grand Rapids: Eerdmans, 1997), pp. 22, 25. While I have learned from Reichenbach's emphasis on teaching as empowerment, I cannot agree with his claim in his paper in this volume that "the professor's function is not to . . . convert, or to make disciples" but simply "to challenge, empower, or free." This language suggests his goal is to render students tradition-less, autonomous thinkers. Yet in the same paragraph he protests Lutheran education that leaves students "less moral and uncommitted to a vision of the truth," which suggests that he wants professors to "convert" students to a way of seeing that is more moral and more committed to the truth. I think the latter statement is closer to his true aim and reflective of what all professors in fact do.

35. Thiessen, *Teaching for Commitment*, pp. 153-54. This is why Diane Scholl rightly argues that "'difference' without a core theology and a set of defining values is doomed to produce a polyglot society that will have trouble functioning as a community, an environment in which respect for the liberal arts . . . flourish[es] and sustain[s] us." Scholl, "Making Dry Bones Stand: Lutheran Higher Education at Century's End," *Intersections* 17 (Summer 2003): 19.

Thus we are closed toward this knowledge that is not accessible to us. It is also apparent, he maintains, that in order to live quotidian life we must make leaps of faith on a regular basis, and come to conclusions which Gordon Kaufman calls "functional absolutes." Therefore we cannot live without believing in some absolutes and closing our minds to certain options.[36]

Should we express neutrality toward every philosophical alternative? Scientists are not neutral toward theoretical alternatives. Far from it. Thiessen cites Karl Popper's claim that tenacity of commitment has played an important role in the history of scientific discovery. "But I have always stressed the need for some dogmatism; the dogmatic scientist has an important role to play. If we give in to criticism too easily, we shall never find out where the real power of our theories lies."[37] As Thiessen argues, we don't call scientists close-minded because they take a position on a question where expert opinion is divided and the evidence ambiguous.[38]

What then is openness if it can be committed to a theory that lacks absolute proof? Let's go back to science. In the case just mentioned, where the evidence is ambiguous, we require scientists who have adopted one of several competing theories to keep an open mind by being willing to reassess their position in light of further research.

In philosophical and religious matters we can do the same. But we must first realize that it is not logically possible to be critical about everything all the time. In Thiessen's words, that's a little like trying to reconstruct a ship while at sea. The problem with critical doubt, he argues, is that it is not critical enough. It does not subject itself to the same doubt. And it does not realize that its critique of tradition and authority is its own authoritative tradition.[39]

We cannot be neutral about everything. And making some exclusive truth claims is unavoidable. But if we are willing to reassess our convictions in the light of new evidence, then we can be committed to religious belief and at the same time have an open and critical mind toward those beliefs.

We need a new concept of critical openness that recognizes both that

---

36. Thiessen, *Teaching for Commitment*, p. 154.

37. Karl Popper, "Normal Science and Its Dangers," in *Criticism and the Growth of Knowledge*, ed. I. Lakatos and A. Musgrove (Cambridge: Cambridge University Press, 1970), p. 55.

38. Thiessen, *Teaching for Commitment*, p. 157.

39. Thiessen, *Teaching for Commitment*, p. 162.

we are not as open as we think and that complete open-mindedness is not optimal or even possible. We should engage in criticism not as an end in itself — for that will lead only to nihilism — but for the sake of understanding and commitment to the truth.

As Thiessen reminds us, the Christian faith encourages not only commitment but also criticism: disciples are told to test the spirits (1 John 4:1), and those in the early church critically evaluated what they were taught against larger paradigms of faith (Acts 17:11). It is also clear from the New Testament that doubt and uncertainty are part of the normal Christian life; Jesus himself struggled with both. Hence commitment to Christian faith is compatible with a proper critical openness.[40]

A New Model: Persuasion and Dialectic

I have tried to make the case that the working model for teaching and learning in the Western intellectual tradition is flawed. In particular, the Enlightenment's presupposition of the possibility of philosophical neutrality is a myth. Hence the bias of many Lutheran college professors against persuasion in the classroom is suspect.

The human person always already thinks and sees from a position of philosophical commitment, even in the sciences but especially when matters of moral or philosophical import are considered. It is therefore impossible to present any subject that touches on moral or philosophical questions with absolute neutrality — or what some would call pure objectivity. Thomas Kuhn showed that science has never proceeded in this cool, detached fashion, and scores of scholars have shown it to be particularly the case in the (more) human sciences.

Therefore one would have to say that all professors seek to persuade. That is, no professor is able to keep her personal convictions entirely separated from what she teaches. Every professor makes value decisions when deciding which subjects to teach, which readings to use, and how to structure a class that investigates a particular subject. Even the notion of getting students to think in different ways about an issue is an attempt to persuade them of the proposition that there is more than one way to approach that issue — or that diversity of approach is better than a single approach. This

---

40. Thiessen, *Teaching for Commitment*, p. 162.

is a moral proposition because it suggests that it is not right to approach life from one position without considering the viewpoints of others. Therefore if persuasion is part of the character of all teaching in the liberal arts, the real question is not whether we persuade but how we do so.

How then shall we persuade? First, I would propose, we can persuade without the guilty feeling that we are corrupting or tainting the learning process by doing so. The truth of the matter is quite the opposite: only by being able to locate a new idea within a "big picture" does the best learning take place. To insist on the methodological principle that religious truth must be separated from other kinds of truth in the classroom — at a Lutheran college of all places — is to diminish the quality of learning. For, as Newman argued, without religious truth one cannot see the fullest extent of any particular truth: "If there be religious truth at all, we cannot shut our eyes to it without prejudice to truth of every kind, physical, metaphysical, historical, and moral; for it bears upon all truth."[41] This does not mean that every course should bring faith into explicit dialogue with its subject matter; but such a dialogue ought not be the exception on campus, nor should it be the exclusive prerogative of the religion and philosophy departments.

Second, we should proceed dialectically. That means we start by proposing a proposition or view of the world that we ask the student to accept on authority — to start with. This "grand idea" gives meaning to many other ideas. It is the big picture into which other, lesser ideas find their place. But we don't stop there. We open the grand idea to challenges. This process is another way of narrating the normative study of myth: by challenging it students find through contradiction a higher truth. We cannot chart the way for the student, and the way is often long, meandering, and unpredictable. It requires and strengthens the highest functions of the mind. Newman captures the intricacies of its crooked way:

> We know, not by a direct and simple vision, not at a glance, but, as it were, by piecemeal and accumulation, by a mental process, by going round an object, by the comparison, the combination, the mutual correction, the continual adaptation, of many partial notions, by the employment, concentration, and joint action of many faculties and exercises of mind.[42]

41. Newman, *Idea of the University,* pp. 88-89.
42. Newman, *Idea of the University,* p. 170.

David V. Hicks describes this model of teaching and learning as "inquiry that reaches into earthly as well as transcendent realms of knowledge."[43] It empowers students to see themselves not as disconnected parts and the universe as a collection of parts but themselves as integral parts of a whole and all parts in relation to the whole. Hence the true teacher is, like Socrates, dedicated to truth, a gadfly who cuts across the grain, trying to instill a desire for truth greater than desire to be proven right, and an inability to fear reason. But the teacher is also one who wants to connect truths to one another and the human self. In other words, a good professor is willing to work amidst the tension between the normative and the utilitarian, the dialectical and the analytical.[44]

I would add that dialectical persuasion must be pursued with fairness, balance, and restraint. By fairness I mean that scholars who learn and teach from a position of faith should not argue on the authority of special or private revelations that many do not accept, but should use scholarly rigor and integrity and treat others with fairness and charity.[45]

By balance I mean that we should take a cue from Stephen Jay Gould, who warns scholars that while they must acknowledge that there is no absolute objectivity, they must not go to the opposite extreme of assuming that objective evidence plays no role in scholarship or that perceptions of truth are entirely relative. What he wrote about science can be said for all learning and teaching: it is a complex dialogue between data and preconceptions.[46]

Finally, restraint means that true persuasion is not indoctrination. Teachers should not coerce but introduce students to claims, practices, and sensibilities that may be new to them. To speak metaphorically, it is our task to lead students to a new country. We should not expect students to change their citizenship but to see and hear and taste a bit of life in that new land. We can ask them to open their eyes and ears to what is truly

43. David V. Hicks, *Norms and Nobility: A Treatise on Education* (Lanham, MD: University Press of America, 1990), p. 66.

44. Hicks, *Norms and Nobility,* pp. 66-77. For a superb analysis of Socrates' pedagogy, see Reichenbach, "On Being a Professor."

45. See George Marsden, "Christian Advocacy and the Rules of the Academic Game," in *Religious Advocacy and American History,* ed. Bruce Kuklick and D. G. Hart (Grand Rapids: Eerdmans, 1997), pp. 3-27, esp. pp. 10, 18.

46. Stephen Jay Gould, *Wonderful Life: The Burgess Shale and the Nature of History* (New York: W. W. Norton, 1989), p. 244; cited in Paul A. Carter, "Seldon's Choice: Variations on a Theme by Asimov," in Kuklick and Hart, eds., *Religious Advocacy,* p. 207.

other, but we must never give them the impression that their grade will be affected by whether or not they change their citizenship.

Nor should we always identify openly our own citizenship. Open profession of our own faith commitment can sometimes distract or hinder the honest wrestling of students with the implications of a faith vision which they are considering — because of the inordinate power a professor wields in the classroom vis-à-vis students. But even if we choose not to reveal our own faith commitment, for the good reason that it might interfere with students' exploration of a new vision, we should not presume that we are no longer persuading. The mere fact that we want students to encounter a new country — if you will — means that we seek to persuade them of the value of such an encounter.

Conclusion

In sum, persuasion is inevitable, particularly in the humanities and social sciences.[47] If done rightly, persuasion can strengthen and deepen learning. Dialectical persuasion, the model proposed in this essay, is not indoctrination. Teaching that inhibits students' growth toward a proper rational autonomy *is* indoctrination, which is immoral. But proper rational autonomy often includes elements that are sometimes carelessly dismissed as "indoctrination." Proper rational autonomy recognizes that we (rightly) depend on others in personal relationships. It can also include uncoerced choices to submit to others, even God. This is procedural autonomy with substantive dependence.

No discipline is more susceptible to indoctrination than another. Every discipline indoctrinates when it does not inform students about its presuppositions and first principles — or opposing perspectives. Without this dynamic inquiry about the foundations of a discipline, or competing ways of looking at the discipline, indoctrination is possible.

Therefore the liberal arts need to be reconceptualized, along its medieval lines, and to rid it of its corrosive tendencies begun by the Enlightenment. We need to liberate the liberal arts from its obsession with searching

---

47. John Milbank argues persuasively that the social sciences are not dispassionate analyses of religion and humanity but crypto-theologies in their own right. John Milbank, *Theology and Social Theory: Beyond Secular Reason* (Oxford: Blackwell, 1993).

at the expense of finding. The age-old tension between the oratorical and philosophical ideals in the liberal arts needs to be restored. The Enlightenment model of education is parasitic — an abstraction from a larger whole. It highlights criticism and suspicion — which are especially healthy in an age of totalisms — but in isolation from traditions that alone can tell us *why* we should be critical. This means, among other things, that a reconstructed liberal arts tradition will initiate students into particular cultures and ways of being as preliminaries to broadening their horizons.

To put this pedagogically, there needs to be a balance between stability and coherence (by teaching a tradition), on the one hand, and criticism of the tradition, on the other. We teachers have our own plausibility structures that provide us with intellectual security. Sometimes we delight in attacking students' plausibility structures, in the interest of liberating them from the present and particular. But a better model would be using the present and particular as a foundation for further growth toward a proper autonomy. A better liberal arts model would complement our sometimes-excessive emphasis on autonomy with attention to nurturing other values such as love, goodwill, benevolence, and harmony.

Finally, we need diversity among *institutions* for a better model of the liberal arts. That is, we need a plurality of schools with different belief systems, each committed to proper rationality and autonomy. Our present system of colleges and universities runs the risk of indoctrinating an entire nation in a rather singular way of looking at life and learning. True pluralism among institutions, representing genuine *intellectual* diversity, will be the best safeguard against the danger of which John Stuart Mill warned: "A general state education is a mere contrivance for moulding people to be exactly like one another. . . . [I]t establishes a despotism of the mind."[48]

48. John Stuart Mill, *On Liberty* (Indianapolis: Hackett, 1978), pp. 104-5; quoted in Thiessen, *Teaching for Commitment*, p. 273. Much of this conclusion was stimulated by Thiessen's analysis, esp. pp. 231-73.

The Recovery of Moral and Religious Truth in the University

DONALD D. SCHMELTEKOPF AND MICHAEL D. BEATY

I

For most of the nineteenth century, American colleges and universities — private as well as state-supported ones — were dominated by a Protestant religious culture. Other important factors were operating as well, such as the practical and economic realities of an expanding nation, but, as George M. Marsden has observed, the cultural hegemony of Protestant leaders at this time was nowhere more evident than in "their gaining control over virtually all the influential colleges in the country, including state schools."[1] This control was signaled not only by the evangelical commitments of many college and university presidents, but also by such markers as required chapel services, attendance at church on Sundays, and substantive Christian teachings in the curriculum, sometimes referred to as "evidences of Christianity." These features would be expected at private universities, but, in fact, state-supported universities were hardly different. As late as 1890, for example, the typical state university in the United States supported compulsory chapel, and that practice did not fade from the scene until the period of World War II.[2]

While required chapel disappeared on state campuses by the middle of the twentieth century, including also at many elite private colleges and uni-

---

1. George M. Marsden, *The Soul of the American University: From Protestant Establishment to Established Nonbelief* (New York: Oxford University Press), p. 4.
2. Marsden, *The Soul of the American University*, pp. 3, 333.

versities, the lingering moral idealism of the Protestant religious culture did not. Standards of student and faculty conduct were strict and enforced virtually everywhere. Curfews for women in women's dormitories were typically at 9:00 p.m. during week nights for freshmen. "Dorm mothers" lived in the dorms to oversee the comings and goings of the young women; young men were kept out except in the guest parlors. Indeed, the widespread assumption held by colleges and universities across the country was that they had an institutional obligation to look after the moral well-being of their students. *In loco parentis* was the settled normative arrangement in higher education into the 1960s. Not only did faculty members have serious obligations in this regard, such as serving as sponsors for student organizations and more generally being role models on campus, so did the wide array of denominational "houses" and "centers" who were invited to look after the religious life of students. Their work even included the offering of religion courses, frequently under the instruction of so-called "Bible chairs," that could serve as electives to fulfill graduation requirements.

However, this moral idealism concealed a more fundamental shift at another level — the secularization of the educational process itself. For much of the first half of the twentieth century, the liberal Protestant culture dominant in higher education across America came to embrace what Marsden has described as "a universal academic ideal, underwritten by Enlightenment assumptions concerning universal science and supported by optimism concerning human nature's ability to progress toward a universal moral ideal."[3] Ironically, this modern notion of what counts as legitimate higher learning meant, for all intents and purposes, that religious perspectives in the American academy would soon be excluded. In fact, by 1950, "normative religious teaching of any sort [had] been nearly eliminated from standard university education."[4] The outcome was an "inclusive" higher education project, one which welcomed all nonsectarian perspectives by excluding religious ones, especially Christian perspectives.

This story of the radical secularization of the academy in America over the last century or so has been vividly chronicled by a number of important studies in the past fifteen years. The most well known of these are George M. Marsden and Bradley J. Longfield, eds., *The Secularization of the American Academy;* George M. Marsden, *The Soul of the American*

---

3. Marsden, *The Soul of the American University*, p. 5.
4. Marsden, *The Soul of the American University*, pp. 4-5.

University; Douglas Sloan, *Faith and Knowledge: Mainline Protestantism and American Higher Education;* Philip Gleason, *Contending with Modernity: Catholic Higher Education in the Twentieth Century;* and James Tunstead Burtchaell, *The Dying of the Light: The Disengagement of Colleges and Universities from Their Christian Churches.* Each of these studies, along with others, makes the point presciently observed by Alasdair MacIntyre in his important work, *Three Rival Versions of Moral Enquiry,* that in the modern university "moral and religious truth ceased to be recognized as objects of substantive enquiry and instead were relegated to the realm of privatized belief."[5] The result has been a crimped and incomplete version of the university.

Our goal in this chapter is to give support to a larger and, in fact, more traditional notion of the university, one that takes into account the full range of human experience, including in particular the moral and religious domains. We will do this from two angles: first, by exploring signs of the recovery of moral and religious truth in the university today, and, second, by making the argument that such a recovery is exactly what is needed for the renewal of the university in American culture — or, to state the matter even more sharply, to overcome the irrelevance of the secular university.[6]

We must say at the outset, however, that one could readily make the claim, with ample warrant, that the secular university has never been more ascendant than it is now. The guardians of virtually all the academic disciplines are deeply embedded in and committed to the specialization, sub-specialization, and sub-sub-specialization of their respective fields. This highly technical and professionalized identity of most disciplines has little or no truck with moral and religious questions. Moreover, when one reads the stated missions of universities today, the one goal expressed by all of them is the secular value of "diversity," diversity not only of background and ethnicity but also of belief.[7] And at the level of student conduct, we

---

5. Alasdair MacIntyre, *Three Rival Versions of Moral Enquiry: Encyclopedia, Genealogy, and Tradition* (Notre Dame, IN: University of Notre Dame Press), p. 217.

6. C. John Sommerville, *The Decline of the Secular University* (Oxford: Oxford University Press, 2006), p. 3.

7. Diversity of belief concerns us particularly. Why should universities, institutions presumably in the business of professing truth, value this form of diversity? Our colleague, Douglas Henry, has suggested that diversity of this sort may be especially prized in a culture that despairs of real truth — provisional or final — because it offers something of a distrac-

hear reports on a regular basis of what only can be described as debauch-ery and binges on the nation's campuses. Tom Wolfe's novel *I Am Charlotte Simmons* vividly depicts such an account at an imaginary elite Southern university, as what one reviewer described as Charlotte's "descent into this University of Hell."[8] In the world of intercollegiate athletics, scarcely a week goes by that we do not hear reports of corruption and fraud. On top of that, the leading football programs in the country, with a few notable ex-ceptions, have graduation rates hovering around 30 percent.

In spite of these and other indications, there is counter evidence today that there is some recovery in the university of what MacIntyre called "moral and theological truth," or what John Henry Newman referred to as "God, nature, and man" when describing the proper curriculum of the university, as noted in his book *The Idea of a University*. To explore ele-ments of counter evidence, we will review three prominent dimensions: at-titudes of students, current literature being published in the field, and cur-ricular developments.

II

One of the truly fascinating trends at the turn of the twenty-first century is the growing influence of religion and spirituality in American life. Na-tional studies prior to this time suggested that many Americans appeared to be losing their religion, hence becoming more secular in their outlook. For example, the General Social Survey and National Election Study showed that from 1988 to 2004, the percentage of Americans who declared that they had no religion rose by slightly over 6 percent, to a total of 14.3 percent of the population. However, the recent Baylor Religion Survey showed that only 10.8 percent were unaffiliated with any religious group, a

---

tion from the hopelessness that otherwise looms so large. Joseph Pieper comments similarly about the apathy that marks despair's bleak manifestation: "In addition to despair, *acedia* gives birth to that uneasy restlessness of mind that . . . reveals itself in loquaciousness *(verbositas)*, in excessive curiosity *(curiositas)*, in an irreverent urge 'to pour oneself out from the peak of the mind into many things' *(importunitas)*, in interior restlessness *(inquietudo)*, and in instability of place or purpose *(instabilitas loci vel propositi)*." See Joseph Pieper, *Faith, Hope, Love* (San Francisco: Ignatius Press, 1997), pp. 120-21.

8. Tom Wolfe, *I Am Charlotte Simmons* (London: Vintage, 2004), back cover quote from *Sunday Times*.

difference that equates to 10 million people. Moreover, according to the Baylor survey, of the so-called unaffiliated, 62.9 percent believe in God or some higher power, and 31.6 percent pray at least occasionally.[9] The overall picture reveals that Americans today may be as religious as ever.

We should not be surprised, therefore, that religion is influencing the attitudes and choices of many college students. For example, from 1990 to 2004, according to the U. S. Department of Education, enrollment in public four-year colleges and universities grew by 12.8 percent, private four-year institutions grew by 28 percent, and religiously affiliated schools grew by 27.5 percent. However, among the 102 member institutions of the Council of Christian Colleges and Universities, the enrollment increase over this same period of time was a staggering 70.6 percent, from 134,592 students to 229,649. Record enrollments in CCCU institutions continued in fall 2005.[10]

In a study by the Higher Education Research Institute at UCLA in 2003, Alexander Astin and his colleagues found that a growing number of students are genuinely interested in religious and spiritual engagement. The report reveals that many college students — as high as three-fourths on some questions — have "very high levels of spiritual interest and involvement, . . . are actively engaged in a spiritual quest and in exploring the meaning and purpose of life. They are also very engaged and involved in religion, reporting considerable commitment to their religious beliefs and practices."[11] While some question the methodology of the HERI study because of the subjective definition of "spirituality,"[12] it is nevertheless the

9. *American Piety in the Twenty-first Century: New Insights to the Depth and Complexity of Religion in the US* (Baylor University, Baylor Institute for Studies of Religion, September 2006), pp. 7-13.

10. http://www.christianpost.com/pages/print.htm?aid=7686.

11. *The Spiritual Life of College Students: A National Study of College Students' Search for Meaning and Purpose* (UCLA, Higher Education Research Institute, 2003), executive summary.

12. Christian Smith offers an important perspective on the subjective aspects of spirituality among America's youth today in his book *Soul Searching: The Religious and Spiritual Lives of American Teenagers* (Oxford: Oxford University Press, 2005). Smith writes: "Here we attempt to summarize our observations by venturing a general thesis about teenage religion and spirituality in the United States. We advance our thesis somewhat tentatively as less than a conclusive fact but more than mere conjecture: we suggest that the *de facto* dominant religion among contemporary U.S. teenagers is what we might call 'Moralistic Therapeutic Deism'" (p. 162).

case that few surveyed identified themselves as "spiritual but not religious." In fact, of the approximately 3,700 students surveyed, 77 percent said they prayed, 71 percent said that their religion was helpful to them, and 73 percent indicated that religious beliefs contributed to shaping their identity. The results of this study are confirmed by an April 2006 poll conducted by Harvard University which "found that seven out of 10 college students consider religion to be important in their lives."[13]

These data suggest, as Robert Connor, president of the Teagle Foundation, wrote in the *Chronicle of Higher Education* recently, that there is widespread interest among college students today in moral and religious truth. In an essay entitled "The Right Time and Place for Big Questions," Connor challenged faculties and administrators in the nation's universities to expand their notions of what should be included within a liberal education. He wrote: "Indeed, some big questions are now front and center in the consciousness of many students. . . . 'What am I going to do with my life?' is often the biggest of the big questions, but there are also questions concerning personal and civic morality, the existence and nature of radical evil, the perennial tug of war between scientific and religious worldviews, and the relationship between wealth and happiness, and between power and justice, in both national and international affairs."[14] From the perspective of the Teagle Foundation, these "big questions" are central to the reinvigoration of the liberal arts in our nation's colleges and universities.

This means that faculty members, as well as administrators, should offer educational leadership to help students reflect on and mature in their religious and spiritual lives. The problem, however, is that the overwhelming majority of faculty members are unprepared to do so, in spite of the fact that almost two-thirds of all faculty members say they are "a religious person," either "to some extent" (29%) or "to a great extent" (35%).[15] Two long-held ideological assumptions within the secular academy have been at work to produce such unprepared faculty members. The first we might call the doctrine of "methodological secularization," the notion that one must assume a non-religious standpoint so that one's disciplinary methods are neutral among competing viewpoints.

13. See W. Robert Connor, "The Right Time and Place for Big Questions," *The Chronicle of Higher Education*, 9 June 2006, p. B8.
14. Connor, "The Right Time and Place," p. B8.
15. *Spirituality and the Professoriate: A National Study of Faculty Belief, Attitudes, and Behaviors* (UCLA, Higher Education Research Institute, 2005), p. 3.

The second assumption at work with most faculty members over the last several decades is the "secularization hypothesis," the notion that with the advent of modernization religion will recede into the background, if not go away altogether, especially on our nation's campuses and in the wider intellectual culture. As one observer of the current scene has stated, "in a time when secularism was prized above all else, it was easy enough for [faculty members] to leave religion and spirituality and the questions they raised at the doorstep of the classroom."[16] This view was confirmed in a recent study (2004-05) by the Higher Education Research Institute on "Spirituality and the Professoriate," in which it was revealed that "nearly two-thirds [of the students] say professors never encourage discussion of spiritual or religious matters."[17] In light of the cataclysmic events surrounding 9/11, as well as the persisting and palpable interest of students in matters of religion and faith, many faculty members now find themselves in an "odd space,"[18] believing that while no one religion seems to be true, it doesn't seem plausible to abandon religious questions and beliefs altogether.

III

Over the past decade, a growing number of scholars, as well as many colleges and universities, both secular and religious, have been trying to sort out appropriate responses to the realities we have described. Sharon Daloz Parks clarifies one aspect of the problem in her work *Big Questions, Worthy Dreams*.

> Since the nineteenth century, and particularly with the development of the research university, higher education has been increasingly dominated by a particular interpretation of academic objectivity that over time has appeared to preclude a self-conscious search for value and meaning. As a result, commitment to the true has been divorced from the question of the good.[19]

16. Cheryl D. Ching, "Religious Work: Report on a Listening," p. 2 (http://www.teaglefoundation.org/learning/report/20051026.aspx).

17. *Spirituality and the Professoriate*, p. 1.

18. Ching, "Religious Work," p. 2.

19. Sharon Daloz Parks, *Big Questions, Worthy Dreams: Mentoring Young Adults in Their Search for Meaning, Purpose, and Faith* (San Francisco: Jossey-Bass, 2000), p. 159.

That is to say, Parks explains, the realm of knowledge has been limited to "objective reality" — empirical fact and its analysis — in contrast to "ultimate reality." This sharp distinction has separated what was known from the knower, "thus diminishing the significance of emotion, intuition, the personal, the moral, and full engagement with the complexity emerging from the practice of lived experience."[20] Within this context, the role of faculty members shifted from the older vision of being mentors to one of being technical experts, enunciating what "the data show" rather than professing a contention or well-considered belief. In the process, students tended to be reduced to either independent, rational thinkers or to novices needing to be awakened to competing estimations of what is known.[21]

One aspect of the phenomenon addressed by Parks is the separation of the education of the intellect, typically regarded as acquiring the competencies necessary for a mastery of objective reality, understood as the natural world, and moral education, which is relegated to the subjective and emotive dimensions of persons and their responses to the world. Yet, many scholars urge a recovery of those texts and traditions that suggest a more unified understanding of reality, of persons, and hence of education, especially with respect to the unity of truth and goodness.[22]

So, it is not surprising that this truncated version of the modern university is increasingly viewed with skepticism, even more, being attacked directly. This can be seen in the critique of scholars like Parks — and more recently by John Sommerville — as well as in several reports from America's campuses about a recovery of interest in moral and religious issues. With respect to the latter, surely the huge increases in enrollment at Christian colleges and universities across the country, noted above, are a telltale sign that students and their parents care deeply not only about what is true, but also about what is good. They are suspicious that secular schools — both public and private — have little or no commitment to this nobler end.

---

20. Parks, *Big Questions*, p. 160.
21. Parks, *Big Questions*, pp. 159-60.
22. See, for example, Robert C. Roberts, "Free Love and Christian Higher Education: Reflections on a Passage from Plato's *Theaetetus*," in *The Schooled Heart: Moral Formation in American Higher Education*, ed. Michael D. Beaty and Douglas V. Henry (Waco, TX: Baylor University Press, 2007), pp. 81-104, for an insightful defense of the view that intellectual and moral education are one thing, not two, and that such a vision stands at the heart of a truly liberal arts university education.

Robert Benne's book *Quality with Soul: How Six Premier Colleges and Universities Keep Faith with Their Religious Traditions* offers a challenge to the secularization of religious colleges by reviewing six case studies that show a significant counter trend. He shows what can and should be done in the face of the modernist tendencies that have swept away the religious connections of many once-Christian institutions, those in which the "light" has died. A different but equally compelling story is told by Naomi Schaefer Riley in *God on the Quad: How Religious Colleges and the Missionary Generation Are Changing America*. Riley wanted to know why it is the case that more and more of America's brightest youth are choosing to attend colleges and universities that uphold both the liberal arts *and* religion. In her investigations at more than a dozen schools, she found that students have been attracted to certain Catholic, Protestant, Jewish, and Mormon schools *precisely because* they take their religious missions seriously. And Larry Braskamp, Lois Trautvetter, and Kelly Ward, in *Putting Students First: How Colleges Develop Students Purposefully*, report on their findings from ten church-related colleges with a specific interest in how these schools help prepare students to live thoughtful lives by: (1) putting students first in their mission; (2) educating students holistically; and (3) dealing with the religious faith dimension in the education of their students.[23]

The renewed interest in moral and religious questions in the American

23. In addition to the works mentioned in this essay, there is considerable other literature available today in the field of religion in higher education. Some examples of these are: Mark Schwehn, *Exiles from Eden: Religion and the Academic Vocation in America* (New York: Oxford University Press, 1992); William H. Willimon and Thomas H. Naylor, *The Abandoned Generation: Rethinking Higher Education* (Grand Rapids: Eerdmans, 1995); George M. Marsden, *The Outrageous Idea of Christian Scholarship* (New York: Oxford University Press, 1997); V. James Mannois Jr., *Christian Liberal Arts: An Education That Goes Beyond* (Lanham, MD: Rowman & Littlefield, 2000); Richard T. Hughes, *How Christian Faith Can Sustain the Life of the Mind* (Grand Rapids: Eerdmans, 2001); Douglas Jacobsen and Rhonda Hustedt Jacobsen, *Scholarship and Christian Faith: Enlarging the Conversation* (New York: Oxford University Press, 2004); Harry Lee Poe, *Christianity in the Academy: Teaching at the Intersection of Faith and Learning* (Grand Rapids: Baker Academic, 2004); Arthur Chickering et al., *Encouraging Authenticity and Spirituality in Higher Education* (San Francisco: Jossey-Bass, 2005); Chris Anderson, *Teaching as Believing: Faith in the University* (Waco, TX: Baylor University Press, 2006); Mark U. Edwards Jr., *Religion on Our Campuses: A Professor's Guide to Communities, Conflicts, and Promising Conversations* (New York: Palgrave Macmillan, 2006); and Douglas Henry and Michael Beaty, eds., *Christianity and the Soul of the University: Faith as a Foundation for Intellectual Community* (Grand Rapids: Baker Academic, 2006).

academy can also be seen in the work of some national professional and educational associations. Three examples will suffice. Perhaps the one of greatest import is the Society of Christian Philosophers, founded about thirty years ago as an affiliated group of the American Philosophical Association. The purpose of the SCP is to explore the nature and role of Christian commitment in philosophy. It has an active current membership of over one thousand and sponsors annual meetings across the country, as well as publishes a journal called *Faith and Philosophy*. A second example can be seen in the activities of the American Assembly of Collegiate Schools of Business, the national accrediting body for schools of business. Particularly since the collapse of Enron and other recent corporate scandals, the AACSB has sponsored several conferences annually on teaching business ethics in our nation's schools of business. The Association of American Colleges and Universities has also entered the field. Recently, it announced the selection of eighteen colleges and universities — from Michigan State to Tulane to University of the Pacific — to lead a new initiative across the nation on educating students for personal and social responsibility.

Not surprisingly, the response that has received the greatest attention is at Harvard, although at this point with uncertain results. As has now been extensively reported in the national and international media, a Task Force on General Education of the Faculty of Arts and Sciences of Harvard University has recommended, in a report issued in February 2007, that all Harvard College undergraduates take courses in eight subject areas to meet the requirements of general education. Two of those areas are "culture and belief" and "ethical reasoning."[24] With regard to courses in culture and belief, the report mandates that such courses should introduce students to important texts, including religious ones, and to an examination of these in light of their historical and cultural contexts. With respect to the study of religion, the report states: "Religious beliefs and practices

24. *Report of the Task Force on General Education,* Copyright 2007 by the President and Fellows of Harvard College, p. 7. This report is a revision of an earlier one, issued on October 3, 2006, which called for a more explicit course requirement in religion, called "Faith and Reason." The co-chair of the task force, Louis Menand, a professor of English, offered this defense of the religion requirement: "I think 30 years ago [when the school's curriculum was last overhauled], people would have said that religion is not something that everyone needs to know. . . . But today, few would disagree that religion is supremely important to modern life." In Zachary M. Seward, "At Harvard, Religion Course May Be Required," *Wall Street Journal,* 5 October 2006, p. D2.

are topics that some courses in this category should address. Religion has historically been, and continues to be, a force shaping identity and behavior throughout the world. . . . [R]eligion is an important part of our students' lives."[25] In fact, the report notes that 71 percent of Harvard's incoming students indicate that they attend religious services.

The requirement in ethical reasoning continues a current requirement in ethics that has been in place in Harvard's general education program for thirty years. The new requirement, however, attempts to connect the ethics requirement more closely to life. "Courses in Ethical Reasoning," the report declares, "teach students to reason in a principled way about moral and political beliefs and practices, and to deliberate and assess claims for themselves about ethical issues." The goal is to link ethical theory (including that based on religion) and practice in a way that students will be more equipped to deal with the ethical dilemmas they "may encounter in their public, professional, and personal lives."[26]

Why did the task force recommend these two areas of study? The fundamental premise of the new curriculum, as noted in the preliminary report of the task force, is that the general education of students should "connect liberal arts education with life." Alison Simmons, professor of philosophy and co-chair of the committee, put it this way in a release from the *Harvard Gazette:* "There was the feeling that the liberal arts need to be defended, and Harvard has to take a stand, on how liberal education changes students and helps them be better people. Once we had that settled, the other things fell into place."[27] And, as the final report concludes: "General education is a statement about why a liberal education matters."[28]

These proposed requirements at Harvard are not, of course, the same kind of religion and ethics requirements — particularly religion — one would typically find at a member school of the Council of Christian Colleges and Universities. That is, for example, a course in "Christian Scriptures" is not going to be required of all students. Nevertheless, surely what is happening at Harvard, along with the other evidences we have mentioned, is a sign that the modern university is reconsidering its long-held

25. *Report of the Task Force on General Education,* p. 11.

26. *Report on the Task Force on General Education,* p. 13.

27. Ruth Walker, "Preliminary Suggestions on General Education," *Harvard University Gazette,* 12 October 2006, p. 2 (http://www.news.harvard.edu/gazette2006/10.12/05-gened.html).

28. *Report of the Task Force on General Education,* p. 24.

view that moral and religious questions are merely private matters, hence not eligible for serious study within the university.

How can one university's action be a sign of this magnitude? For two reasons: one, because Harvard is the oldest and arguably most prestigious university in the United States, and, two, because the intellectual climate at Harvard, for good or ill, is often a barometer of the intellectual climate nationally. What Harvard does, even in the area of general education, frequently sets the direction that other colleges and universities will follow, including especially the most elite ones. This was the case with the last two reforms of general education that came out of Harvard. In 1945, James Bryant Conant, then president, instituted a curriculum reform known simply as the "Red Book" which called for an emphasis on civic values in undergraduate education. The "Red Book" was widely read in colleges and universities across the country. In fact, we recall our own excitement in reading the report in the early 1970s. It was at this time, however, that Harvard reformed its general education again, adopting an "approaches to knowledge" theme. Within a decade, one college after another, as well as higher education associations, began to embrace a "ways of learning and knowing" model for general education. Whether or not the Faculty of Arts and Sciences adopts this most recent plan, the truth is that the national conversation about moral and religious questions prompted by Harvard's initiative will very likely be a significant challenge to the long-held "secularization hypothesis" in the secular academy.

But what Harvard is now recommending about the core curriculum for undergraduates did not occur in a vacuum. A number of intellectual currents and other curricular initiatives have taken place over the last two decades or more that are part of the context. On the intellectual side, many of the most important scholarly contributions today are being made at points where disciplines intersect. This fact gives legitimacy to the attempt to move away from traditional disciplinary foundations for general education to interdisciplinary approaches. In addition, knowledge today is often seen as "perspectival," suggesting that one's ideological commitments, beliefs, and particular experiences of life will inevitably come into play in many educational and intellectual endeavors. If feminist or naturalist perspectives are welcomed, how can religious ones not be?

Moreover, applied ethics courses today appear everywhere in professional schools across the country. In fact, in light of management fraud in companies such as Enron, WorldCom, and Tyco, and accounting scandals in firms such as Adelphia Communications, Global Crossing, and even Xerox, and the role played in these scandals by firms such as Arthur Andersen, more and more professional organizations are requiring ethics modules or courses as a condition of licensure in given professional fields. In Texas, for example, the Texas State Board of Public Accountancy has amended its licensure rules to require that all applicants for the CPA exam complete an approved three-semester-hour college course in ethics. And, interestingly, in the field of hotel management, we have direct knowledge of a thriving faith-based course now being offered in the Dedman School of Hospitality at Florida State University entitled, "Business Ethics and Moral Leadership." The course description reads in part as follows: "This course will focus on the intersections between business and religious ethics, and especially on the ways biblical principles and themes are developed by selected Christian and Jewish writers."[29] This at a major state university!

IV

In *The Decline of the Secular University* John Sommerville makes a startling claim. He argues that the secular university is increasingly marginal in our American culture precisely because it is secular.[30] As a consequence of their secularism, says Sommerville, such universities fail to connect with human beings' "deepest interests and most pressing concerns,"[31] thus making the secular university increasingly irrelevant to American society. Indeed, Sommerville claims that the ideological secularization of Western universities has produced truncated universities, that is, universities that are less than they ought to be. Ironically, Sommerville claims that the secularization of the university has harmed American universities and colleges more than secularization has harmed the society and culture universities serve.

These are bold and complex claims. Some are essentially empirical; others essentially normative. We have already shown that American soci-

---

29. "Business Ethics and Moral Leadership," Florida State University, course syllabus, fall semester, 2006. Provided by Robert A. Brymer, Dedman School of Hospitality.

30. Sommerville, *The Decline of the Secular University*, p. 4.

31. Sommerville, *The Decline of the Secular University*, p. 6.

ety continues to be very religious, despite the ideological secularism of our culture's most prestigious universities and the secularism of some our society's dominant institutions — the news media, the entertainment industry, and the major political parties. The religiosity of mainstream America is so striking a fact that a prominent secular historian, David Hollinger of Stanford, recently asserted that historians and sociologists need to study this phenomenon seriously.[32] He lamented that the intellectuals (like himself, of course) win all the arguments but lose in the court of public opinion, and asked, why are the views of the intellectuals so marginal to public belief and practice? And, of course, this is Sommerville's point.

We want to distinguish two claims that we find confused by Sommerville in his book, a book we greatly admire. The first is the claim that the secular university is increasingly marginal to the American culture. The second is the claim that ideological secularism has harmed the university, with the consequence that the secular university is much less than a university ought to be. The first is essentially an empirical claim and evaluating its ultimate truth or falsity will be quite a complicated task, one beyond our powers.

But we are skeptical of that claim. At first blush, the secular university does not appear to be marginal to our American culture, despite the impressive facts that Sommerville cites. Indeed, one might argue that the secular university is to our society what the Catholic Church was to Christendom in the medieval era. While the secular university may not baptize our children, it initiates, even catechizes them into our culture's essential practices — methodological skepticism, hedonistic materialism, and acquisitive capitalism. As we previously indicated, *I Am Charlotte Simmons* is not far off in its depiction of the banality and debauchery that is considered normative in many colleges and universities. We may wish the modern university were irrelevant, given the secular harms it makes possible, but the truth seems to be otherwise, at least in comparison with what would be the case were the university true to itself, traditionally understood.

Regarding Sommerville's claim that ideological secularism has harmed the university, we believe on this matter he is altogether persuasive. The former pope, John Paul II, begins his encyclical *Fides et Ratio: On the Relationship of Faith and Reason* with the following beautiful metaphor.

---

32. Sommerville, *The Decline of the Secular University*, p. 4.

Faith and reason are like two wings on which the human spirit rises to the contemplation of truth; and God has placed in the human heart a desire to know the truth — in a word, to know himself — so that, by knowing and loving God, men and women may also come to the fullness of truth about themselves (cf. Ex 33:18; Ps 27:8-9; 63:2-3; John 14:8; 1 John 3:2).[33]

In this passage, John Paul II reminds his readers that our lives may be understood as a journey toward truth, a journey for which both faith and reason are necessary co-laborers. The journey would ideally include appropriation of truths of various kinds: truths about particular aspects or parts of reality, truths about how these partial truths fit into larger and more comprehensive understandings of nature and the cosmos, and truths that answer questions about the ultimate meaning of human existence, ultimately leading us toward an absolute, "something ultimate which might serve as the ground of all things."[34]

The late Pontiff claims that the more we human beings understand reality and the world, the more we understand ourselves as human beings and as individuals.[35] As John Paul II sees the matter, the search for truth includes the recognition that there are different modes of truth or ways of knowing and thus different methods of inquiry. Some are the methods employed in everyday life and in scientific experimentation and confirmation. Some are moral truths whose discernment may require a morally well-formed character within which the capacity for moral discernment becomes a power manifest in some moral exemplars but not in others. Some are speculative inquiries into cosmology and metaphysics; these are necessarily philosophical with the results often intrinsically linked to theological truths. Moreover, neither philosophy nor science, when properly pursued, are enemies of theological truths, because faith and reason both aim at a truth that comes from a common source.[36] So, even when reason prepares the way for the apprehension of the truths of faith, reason —

---

33. John Paul II, *Fides et Ratio: On the Relationship Between Faith and Reason* (Boston: St. Paul Books and Media, 1998), p. 7.

34. John Paul II, *Fides et Ratio*, p. 40.

35. John Paul II, *Fides et Ratio*, p. 9.

36. John Paul II, *Fides et Ratio*, pp. 49-65. In these pages, John Paul II discusses the essential complementary relationship between faith and reason and the negative consequences of abandoning this conception.

whether in the form of philosophy, scientific inquiry, or theology — is intrinsically and not merely instrumentally valuable.[37]

In *Three Rival Versions of Moral Enquiry*, MacIntyre suggests that we answer the question, "What are universities for?" by asking, "What peculiar goods do universities serve?" This latter question requires us to specify the peculiar and essential function(s) which no other institution than the university is equipped to do.[38] John Paul II's sweeping vision suggests that the university is that institution whose principal function is to order a variety of intellectual modes of inquiry so that we human beings might better understand ourselves and all of reality. The ultimate aim is a wide and deep notion called understanding or wisdom. Since the attainment of understanding depends on a variety of methods of inquiry oriented to differing modes of truth in the natural sciences, the social sciences, and the humanities, a genuine university will be a place that honors and orders these various methods of inquiry and the modes of truth to which such inquiries provide us access.[39] Clearly, a student who attends a university of this sort participates in his or her transformation from what one is into the fullness of one's actual capacities as a human being.

Later in the encyclical, John Paul II lists a variety of practices and modes of inquiry whose aim is understanding or wisdom. In doing so, the late Pontiff reminds us of philosophy's original meaning as the love of wisdom. His account presumes (1) the unity of truth and goodness, and (2) that wisdom includes knowledge of God, or theology, both natural and revealed. Thus, on John Paul II's view, philosophy and theology are both essential and constitutive features of a genuine university, one that is true to its original and most important purposes and one that presumes in its practices the unity of truth and goodness.

But the story of the modern university, told so well by Julie Rueben in

---

37. John Paul II, *Fides et Ratio*, pp. 42-48.

38. MacIntyre, *Three Rival Versions of Moral Inquiry*, p. 222.

39. What we infer from John Paul II about the distinctive aim of the university includes but goes beyond the answer MacIntyre gives in *Three Rival Versions of Moral Inquiry*. In it, MacIntyre asserts that the specifying feature of the university is to be the place where conceptions and standards of rational justification are developed, applied in a variety of forms of rational inquiry, and then further evaluated so that the wider society can learn how to conduct its own debates, theoretical or practical, in rationally defensible ways (p. 222). In our view, MacIntyre is correct, but these forms of rational inquiry serve the further goods or ends of understanding and wisdom.

her book *The Making of the Modern University: Intellectual Transformation and the Marginalization of Morality*,[40] is the marginalization of theology and philosophy, especially with respect to the notion that there are theological and moral truths. Three significant movements precipitated their marginalization. First, the success of science suggested to some that all genuine knowledge must conform to scientific practices and methods of inquiry and confirmation. After determined but failed efforts by many Protestant liberals to make all theological or moral truth empirical, these claims were relegated to the private and subjective. If the university is constituted by nothing but various forms of empirical inquiry, then theological and moral truths are out of place, so some maintained.

Second, the modern university became linked to human material progress by technological success grounded in scientific advances. Thus, the university increasingly became viewed as essential to human progress, though for purely instrumental reasons. As government and big business invested heavily in the university, and as middle-class Americans increasingly sent their children to the university so they might achieve economic and political success, the university's instrumental or utilitarian value was viewed as obvious. Finally, the professionalization and hyper-specialization of the disciplines privileged the technical and the professional or career-oriented education over other older, more comprehensive and speculative modes of inquiry and their emphases on the acquisition of wisdom. Thus, philosophy and theology were further marginalized. As we suggested earlier in this chapter, serious discussion of theological and moral truths in the American university curriculum began to disappear a century ago, a movement that was completed by the middle of the twentieth century. Other than in denominationally connected institutions, such discussions tended to be relegated to extra-curricular opportunities associated with religious experiences.

We contend that there are no good philosophical arguments that place theological and moral truths, or more generally, the desire for wisdom, outside the purposes of the university — any university! Certainly, there are prominent scholars who defend a view of the university that is shorn of its original commitments to moral and religious education.[41] For

---

40. Julie Reuben, *The Making of the Modern University: Intellectual Transformation and the Marginalization of Morality* (Chicago: University of Chicago Press, 1996).

41. See Richard Rorty's comments in Richard Rorty, Julie A. Reuben, and George Mars-

example, David Hollinger has recently insisted that critics of the present state of university education should not advocate that moral and religious formation be included as aims of the university. He insists that the only goal of undergraduate education is intellectual excellence.[42] But he provides no argument and his view presupposes the decline in the university that we have discussed.[43] A university, true to its original and still compelling purposes, includes these kinds of inquiries and is incomplete without them. A university that is true to its calling, whether it acknowledges its calling or not, will then embrace an older and more comprehensive understanding of the university, something on the order of that suggested by John Paul II.

Any university that takes such a calling seriously will almost certainly have to make radical changes in its current practices. For example, a more unified curriculum, one that truly provides all students with a genuine liberal arts education, will be necessary. This curriculum will perforce include the serious pursuit of moral and religious questions. Thus, given the prevailing practices in most colleges and universities today, a university true to its calling will be counter-cultural, at least for a time. If Sommerville and others are correct, that kind of education will be precisely what meets our students' "deepest interests and most pressing concerns." The mission of the so-called secular university, therefore, need not be fundamentally different from the Christian university. All universities should pursue the goal of wisdom. The distinctive role of the Christian university

---

den, "The Moral Purposes of the University: An Exchange," *The Hedgehog Review* 2, no. 3 (Fall 2000): 106-19. See also Stanley Fish, "Why We Built the Ivory Tower," *New York Times*, 21 May 2004, p. A23.

42. David Hollinger, "Enough Already: Universities Do Not Need More Christianity," in *Religion, Scholarship, and Higher Education: Perspectives, Models and Future Prospects: Essays from the Lilly Seminar on Religion and Higher Education*, ed. Andrea Sterk (Notre Dame, IN: University of Notre Dame Press, 2002), p. 48. Notice that Hollinger's claim presumes that moral and religious formation has nothing to do with intellectual excellence, a peculiarly modern presumption.

43. Numerous practical difficulties face any college or university that takes seriously not only intellectual excellences but also the moral and religious formation of its students. For an extended discussion not only of the practical difficulties such a project included, but also the philosophical case for it, see Michael D. Beaty and Douglas V. Henry, eds., *The Schooled Heart: Moral Formation in American Higher Education* (Grand Rapids: Baker Academic, 2006), especially "Retrieving the Tradition, Remembering the End," by Beaty and Henry.

is to be ever-faithful to its calling and in so doing help provide clarity, as an exemplar, to all universities regarding their true mission.

We have argued that current forms of education prevailing at secular and religious institutions are incomplete and fail to meet students' deepest interests and most pressing concerns. We take it that the report from Harvard University's Taskforce on General Education, and the extensive literature we have cited, provides confirming evidence for our thesis — that a university education is essentially related to the human desire for wisdom and that, as Sommerville suggests, such a quest is inherently religious. It is no surprise, then, that Harvard's next effort at general education will include as a component the effort to expose students to vital religious texts as well as to the normative reasoning associated with the moral life. Whether their programmatic strategies are effective, the aim is on target.

The splendid mandate of Christian colleges and universities today, institutions such as Baylor University, Boston College, Georgetown University, Pepperdine University, and the University of Notre Dame, is to take the lead in being universities serious about the pursuit of moral and religious truth — to be about the goal of wisdom, properly grounded!

Religious Perspectives on Democratic Capitalism

Joseph A. Swanson

Bob Benne has proven a thoughtful and courageous Lutheran theologian for some four and one-half decades. He does not shy from difficult themes. In so doing he has consistently challenged extant thinking and found a way to argue his case consistently with Luther's own constructions.[1] Christians of all churches have found his counsel of great use. Critical, I think, to understanding Benne's contributions is this: he takes up topics of great import and vigorously works his way into new thought arenas, often to the reconstruction of prior debates. In that his work has proven so insightful, we need Benne's work to provide the discernment that most could not find.

In *The Ethic of Democratic Capitalism* (1980) we have a case in point: here Benne considers economic ethics from a Lutheran perspective, resulting in a *tour de force* in its singular construction. This is a careful explication of free market capitalism (replete with Niebuhrian qualifications, calling for government intervention), and an exhausting measurement (yes, call it exacting evaluation) based on John Rawls's criteria enumerated in *A Theory of Justice* (1971).

Now think on this: Benne, teaching at the relatively unnoticed Lutheran School of Theology at Chicago (within sight of the Frank Knight–inspired and Hayek-minded Chicago economics department) jumps into the fray of economic and political debate. He has Luther's theology well in

---

1. Robert Benne, *The Ethic of Democratic Capitalism* (Minneapolis: Fortress Press, 1980).

hand, but he is over his head with market capitalism, and he knows that any Lutheran kid as new to this world as he is needs some metrics to evaluate what he is learning. Tough stuff this! And how does he approach it? With the energy of a single-wing quarterback from West Point, Nebraska: smart thinking, careful blocking, and an occasional "spin move," resulting in either a touchdown scored or a significant improvement in field position. If one had to do in economic theory what Benne was required to do on that football field, then this masterful intellectual achievement was just "a piece of cake."

I will deal with *The Ethic of Democratic Capitalism* in its three elements below, and conclude with where I think the field has been tending, with some comments on issues that need addressing.

Temporal Background: Economics and Theology

I belong to a group of religious intellectuals whose current political and theological thinking was formed out of a mix of moderate Democrat to left-wing socialist families. The setting was the 1970s. Social justice, with special attention to matters of labor organization and income as well as wealth redistribution, was at the top of the political catechism. We were excited about the retirement of Dwight David Eisenhower and the election of the youthful John Fitzgerald Kennedy. That new administration appointed Harvard professors McGeorge Bundy (no less than the Dean of Faculties), John Kenneth Galbraith, and Arthur M. Schlesinger Jr. to positions that appeared to signal new directions in domestic and international policy.[2]

The religious intellectuals who would become neoconservatives would be numerous by the mid-1970s. At its lead were these: Robert Benne, Richard John Neuhaus, and Michael Novak.[3] Those of a more sec-

2. How poorly we read between the lines! Only Bundy had a position of power. Galbraith was sent as ambassador to India (where he tried, without success, via diplomatic channels to influence both domestic policy and international relations). Schlesinger was the saddest case of the three, for he was given an office in the East Wing along with Mrs. Kennedy's staff. Denied requisite security clearances, his constant stream of memorandums to the President were not even filed.

3. In 1982 Michael Novak published a book of similar title, but differing constructions: *The Spirit of Democratic Capitalism* (New York: Simon & Schuster, 1982). By not dealing with

ular bent, but not without a full understanding of the Judaeo-Christian intellectual traditions, would include Irving Kristol and Norman Podhoretz. I was for decades a fringe member of the group, for I wrote nothing on the signal topics.

There were very few, if any, economists in our earlier set of friends. I was already on the slippery slope toward what I did, and still do, call *free market capitalism*. My choice of obtaining a Ph.D. in economics was strongly influenced by a conversation with Milton Friedman. In this man I found a non-religious Jew, who had a new catechism: based in price theory, fully understanding the need for "safety nets" for the unemployed, with an understanding that monetary policy called for an active federal government role in the economy.

Per "Brother Friedman," I was not alone. Benne, in particular, was Chicago-located, adjacent to the University of Chicago. He was a regular player on that university's faculty club tennis courts, where Friedman and George Stigler played alongside his matches with the then start-up genius of financial economics, Eugene Fama. It would follow that Benne found access to the best minds in free market economics on a regular basis. From those days in the mid-1970s would spring the conception of *The Ethic of Democratic Capitalism*.

Since the end of the Great War, economics and theology had been thoroughly separated. While the institutional economics tradition staggered on, its collective set of works was not well developed.[4] Wesley C. Mitchell, founder of the National Bureau of Economic Research, with great effort and the enthusiastic recruitment of giants like Arthur Burns and Simon Kuznets, compiled a solid set of macroeconomic data. These data would prove the basis for exploratory work on economic growth, business cycles, capital formation and financing, and productivity performance. By the end of the 1930s John Hicks and Paul Samuelson, working independently — and divided by the expanse of the Atlantic Ocean — would rework Alfred Marshall's classic theory of price determination, in a field to be called neoclassical microeconomics. Very little in these two develop-

---

Novak's work on this topic I do not mean to minimize his contributions. I am writing here about Benne, not about the estimable Novak.

4. Kenneth Boulding, once considered an institutional economist, is rumored to have said this: institution economics is a collection of bad economics, bad political science, and bad sociology — all gathered by personal bias.

ments would touch upon the enlightenment themes raised by Adam Smith: the distribution of wealth, and the causes of economic growth.[5]

The Ethic of Democratic Capitalism: Roots, Conclusions, and Intellectual Sustainability

So there was Benne in Hyde Park, say in 1974, asking some hard questions. Let me suggest that they were these: (1) How does income get distributed? (2) How does income grow most rapidly? (3) To provide rapid increases in national income, which organization of economic activity accomplishes that best? (4) What are the welfare consequences of alternative organizational forms, and — most critically — how does society provide for the consequences of rapid economic growth that prove, most frequently, disruptive of the lives of those who labor in the vineyards?

These questions, asked and addressed in Benne's *Ethic of Democratic Capitalism*, are amazing, for they bring together the concerns of Adam Smith in *The Wealth of Nations* — and especially those of his prior tome, largely unread to this day, *The Theory of Moral Sentiments*.

The elements of capitalism were pretty well documented when Benne began his research. Harvard's Joseph Schumpeter had defined the record of its European and American results and made a forecast of its constant (though important) instability. John Kenneth Galbraith, more a magazine essayist than an economist, had offered up a vision of failing monopoly capitalism that could be propped up with regulations devised by the tenured faculty of the Harvard economics department.

Well, what then in 1980, did Benne have to offer? A whole lot, I suggest, but I will be brief:

- The best way to provide for economic growth is to provide a functional legal structure for competitive performance.
- This structure must pay attention to property rights — for those who invest in promising technologies must have their physical and intellectual property rights assured by a supportive government. Not only a government regulatory régime that protects franchise rights of extant

---

5. That said, one can see Kuznets (early on) starting to assemble data in lattice work that would provide answers to these issues.

firms, but one that allows open competition for new product designs and process implementation.

- There is a role for government to assist (some) workers, and not capitalists, in adaptation to the dynamics of a capitalist market.[6] I think of this as agape love in the Christian tradition.[7]

One can deduce much from this set of prescriptions. But the most certain set of deductions is this: Benne got the economic system bet right, the first time in a long time that a theologian had done so in this field. Courageously, he used the Rawls system of appraisal of results, one that economists had yet to take up. When Rawls's concept of the *social contract* was taken up, it did not survive well. That initial debate came not from an economist, but from his Harvard philosophy colleague, Robert Nozick.[8] I have lightly mulled over Nozick's deconstruction of Rawls's work, but will conjecture this: Benne's vision of the marketplace — its rewards and failures — would meet the tests of social contracts that Nozick provides.

Economics and Theology: Where These Are Engaged at the Beginning of the Twenty-first Century

Well, much has changed in economics and theology in the last decade. Let me begin with economics.

Max Weber, a genius social scientist at the turn of the nineteenth cen-

---

6. I cannot find a reference in Benne's *Ethics of Democratic Capitalism* to this, but I can read between the lines. To my mind, it goes this way: capitalists are "them that bet," and they have access to very high expected rates-of-return on their investments. Should they fail, they are most likely uninformed and need to learn from the experience. Per the workforce, it is a different matter, for they tend to be less informed on the technological prospects of the venture that employs them. But let us divide that workforce into two segments: risk-takers and job-seekers. The former have a rough understanding of the sector in which they will be playing, and often a shared-bet with their employer. It follows that they need not receive government support for the bets they have made (read insurance against losses). But the latter, most likely undereducated, are just folks working their way in the labor market. They need some temporary support in their search for a job.

7. The best restatement of the *agape* love concept is to be found in Benedictus XVI, *Deus Caritas Est*, December 12, 2005.

8. Robert Nozick, *Anarchy, State and Utopia* (New York: Basic Books, 1974).

tury, had a set of hypotheses that went to the Protestant Reformation's impact on economic growth. At the heart of these was the underlying work ethic of Protestants in the kingdoms where they were employed or managed firms. Economic historians, and (as a result) economists, forgot about Weber's constructions. Being trained in economics at this time, I can understand how the extant paradigm (focused on the efficient organization of production) had little time for "culture." Weber has had an important reintroduction into the economics curriculum.[9]

The constant growth of output in capitalist economies brought to economics a need for a better understanding of that process. Robert Solow in 1960 found that high rates of labor productivity increase could not be understood by watching the addition of capital-labor ratios.[10] Eventually, the classical notion of diminishing returns would put too much capital in the hands of too few workers — and the productivity of the latter would decline. Solow offered up a multiplier effect: on average, if product [denoted by $Q(t)$] exceed product in the prior year, $Q(t-1)$ then it could only be explained by a scalar multiple, $A(t)$. And from where could that multiple have arisen? He called it "technical change." In short order, economists would be looking for the fairly regular increase in that $A(t)$ function.[11]

Along came Douglass North, with some prescriptive understandings of this phenomenon. Looking across countries, he determined that cultural factors figured more than heavily in productivity growth, the short-term for Solow's $A(t)$ function. Well, we have the "nut of the problem" here. But what are the cultural factors? Look across Northern Europe, then south to the "low countries" and northern Germany, and what does one find? Straightforwardly, property rights and a judicial system that supports these — together with open labor markets, and agreed (and enforceable) contracts between workers and their employers. We economists now call the field that North created the *new institutional economics*.

This branch of economics takes us into so many key elements of an economy's functioning: contracts, trust, and incentives. And in short order they take us to religion, which sits at the base of these actions. It proves that we should have not marked down Weber. Watch for the ongoing re-

9. See this from the estimable Stanley Engerman: "Max Weber, *The Protestant Ethic and the Spirit of Capitalism* — Review Essay." http://eh.net/bookreviews/library/engerman.

10. Robert Solow, "Technical Change and the Aggregate Production Function," *The Review of Economics and Statistics* 39 (1957): 312-20.

11. Quite simply, $A(t)$ has a first derivative that is greater than or equal to one.

search of Robert Barro[12] and the special insights of Deirdre McCloskey,[13] for they are telling.

I write now of modern-day theology, in relation to the themes of the marketplace. There is no better place to begin than in Pope John Paul II's encyclical letter *Centesimus annus*.[14] And what do we find here?

With respect to the market system:

- a most full appreciation for property rights and a legal system to support these;
- the requirement of attention to those displaced by the dynamics of capitalism;
- freedom of expression for the participants in these markets, most specially those where labor contracts are negotiated.

Have I missed something? If not, in 1980 Robert Benne brought to the great debate about political economy a more systematic analysis than any other theologian to date. He saw the divides; he sought earnestly to outline the possible constructive outcomes consistent with a Christian ethos. In his own language he is an ordinary saint, and the best of them.

12. Rachel M. McCleary and Robert J. Barro, "Religion and Economy," *Journal of Economic Perspectives* 20 (2006): 49-72.

13. Deirdre N. McCloskey, *The Bourgeois Virtues: Ethics for an Age of Commerce* (Chicago: University of Chicago Press, 2006).

14. John Paul II, *Centesimus annus*, May 1, 1991. (Note the date.)